All of Life Redeemed

"*All of Life Redeemed* is a great little book to put in the hands of the present student generation, indeed, of all young people. This is a kind of primer of systematic Christian thinking. Its style and many telling illustrations are an idiom with which contemporary students and young people feel at home. But the book is true to God's self-revelation in Jesus Christ, who came proclaiming the coming of the Kingdom. It drives home the magnificence of the scope of the deliverance Christ brings—wide as creation itself; and it shows how redemption in its full biblical sense gives meaning to every aspect of our everyday lives and intellectual enterprises."

—*Dr. H. Evan Runner,*
Professor of Philosophy Emeritus,
Calvin College, Grand Rapids, Michigan

"Out of their experience as Christian communicators to students and young adults, the authors have brewed a lively mix of thoughts on what true faith requires in the way of a changed lifestyle.

"Punchily probing beyond platitudes, they offer us vision, imagination and provocation by turns as they explain how ordinary lives gain extraordinary worth and dignity through sharing in God's new order. This book will keep you awake, force you to think, build you up and make you wise."

—*Dr. J.I. Packer,*
Author of Knowing God,
Professor of Historical and Systematic Theology,
Regent College, Vancouver, British Columbia

"This is interesting, helpful and fresh reading for the Christian grappling with what it means to have a life-world-view."

—*R.C. Sproul,*
President and Founder of
the Ligonier Valley Study Center,
Stahlstown, Pennsylvania

All of Life Redeemed

Biblical Insight for Daily Obedience

Bradshaw Frey
William Ingram
Thomas E. McWhertor
William David Romanowski

PAIDEIA PRESS
Jordan Station, Ontario, Canada

The publisher would like to express appreciation for permission to quote from the *Holy Bible: New International Version*, copyright © 1978 by the New York International Bible Society. Used by permission of Zondervan Bible Publishers.

Cover design by Bonnie LaVallee.

ISBN 0-88815-151-9
Printed in Canada.

Foreword

W hat makes this book something significant and different among publications written from an evangelical
perspective? In my view the following points are especially
noteworthy.

All of Life Redeemed, as its title indicates, takes seriously
the *comprehensive* scope of the claims of the gospel. It emphasizes and illustrates that redemption in Jesus Christ has
implications for the entirety of human life—in its personal,
societal and cultural dimensions—and indeed for the whole
earthly creation in which mankind has been placed to serve
God. Another way of making the same point is to say that the
authors constantly emphasize and reaffirm two basic biblical
themes which the dominant secular culture of the West takes
great pains to deny or ignore: the themes of creational ordinances and of spiritual warfare, both cosmic in scope. In a
word, this book seeks to take seriously the titanic *battle for
creation* between the Lamb and the Dragon, and to bring this
understanding to bear on the everyday life of people living in
the industrialized societies of the West. Thus, its first
strength and distinctive significance lies in the *integrality* of
its perspective, the steady and persistent opposition, not only
to outright secular humanism, but also to all Christian views
of the world which seek in some way to limit the scope and
radical significance of creation, sin and grace.

The book's second signal strength lies in its thorough
embeddedness in American culture—that is to say, in the
culture at the center of the world-wide American empire. For
this reason, the book can oppose American secularized

culture from within; in so doing, it provides much-needed guidance for all Christians living within the orbit of that culture throughout the world. And this guidance is not only negative. The authors seek to provide positive Christian direction in the context and at the very heart of secular culture. They critique the movies, the popular songs, the television programs, the advertising and the business practices of contemporary America; they draw their illustrations from these and other sectors of popular culture; they suggest biblical directives for Christian renewal in these areas. In all these ways, the authors are applying the medicine of the gospel at the strategic center of a globally influential cultural movement. In the full sense of the word, this book deserves to be called *reformational*, for it works from an integral biblical perspective for a renewal-from-within of our everyday life in service of God.

A third strong point is the authors' use of Scripture. The Bible comes alive when it is allowed to shed its revealing light on *all* the creational paths that the human race is called to seek out and walk upon before the face of Yahweh. Here the searchlight of Scripture scans a wide range of human tasks and responsibilities. And reference to Scripture is made with an exegetical tact, a naturalness, an easy familiarity and assurance, which serves rather than obstructs the native authority and perspicuity of the Word of God. Nor is this use of Scripture facile or simplistic: it is based on serious study and responsible exegesis, taking seriously the historical and canonical context of the passages cited. It is undoubtedly this extensive and confident use of Scripture which gives the book its persuasiveness and compelling force.

Finally, the book derives its quality of immediacy and authenticity from the context in which it arose. Each of the four authors have belonged for some years to the staff of the Coalition for Christian Outreach, a young and vigorous organization for student ministry based in Pittsburgh, Pennsylvania. Scores of dedicated young men and women serve on dozens of campuses scattered in a wide circle around Pittsburgh, working in various capacities which enable them to bring the gospel and its implications to the students of today. Because the Coalition takes seriously not only its evangelistic task, but also the cultural context and academic calling of the students it reaches, it has developed a broad and holistic ministry. It is this ministry, with the communication skills it has fostered, which has made this book possible. And since the college student can in many ways be taken as the typical of the proverbial "intelligent layman," this book speaks directly to the concerns not only of Christian students, but to those of a far wider range of Christians, whether young or old in the faith, who have caught a glimpse of the far-reaching ramifications of that basic Christian confession: "Jesus is Lord."

—Dr. Al Wolters,
Senior Member in the History of Philosophy,
Institute for Christian Studies, Toronto

Contents

Introduction

When a new person is introduced into a group of people who already know each other (perhaps at a crowded fraternity party or a family reunion), he or she meets a rush of introductory questions: "What's your major?" "Where are you from?" This book enters a densely populated world of "books on the Christian Life," and so it needs introduction.

Those responsible for a new work must feel that their book fills a specific need in a special way. As John Wesley desired the union of faith and knowledge within the lives of early Methodists, so our desire is to see personal devotion to Jesus as Savior and Lord united with faith which finds biblical expression in our culture. We have come to maturity and we seek to work in a world so broken and needy that sometimes we feel hopeless. Can we hope for nothing better than escape ("Christ against culture" as Richard Neibuhr puts it)? No. The record of God's dealing with His people challenges us to faithful obedience *in* culture. We can cooperate with God's Spirit in our age as God's people have done in ages past, and so we may provide the raw materials for reclaiming the Kingdom of the rightful King.

Around the world, the body of Christ suffers fragmentation. In one cultural setting the Christian ideal is to seek God's blessing through financial prosperity. In another, the gospel propels believers to revolution against the existing economic and political order. Our desire is to find some common ground for common endeavor. We feel that the rugged individualism often espoused in church circles does not give adequate emphasis to a community of believers seeking to know the mind of Christ. Our own efforts here retain unique aspects of personal style, highlighting a variety of personalities, and yet we each submit our understanding of God's Word to the light of the experiences and insights of others.

The book begins by examining the world as God created it and the impact and effects of sin on that world (1). Where there is sin, there must be redemption before life can be lived in harmony with God; Christ's role as mediator is central to a clear understanding of redemption (2). In turn, restoration in Christ (3), which is often misunderstood today, draws its meaning from this redemption. Future restoration has present implications for servants in the restored Kingdom. Servanthood (4), a demand made upon all believers, provides a thematic stepping stone to "Daily Obedience in the Activities of Life" (5 and 6). The panorama of our lives can be appreciated in its scope and variety only when seen as a part of God's present and future Kingdom (7).

The need for a work which tries to bring the assurance and drama of the gospel to our daily, ordinary life setting becomes clearer as our culture races to its own destruction, in spite of increasing numbers who claim allegiance to God. One commentator, citing figures from a 1982 survey, concludes, "More people favor prayer in school than participate in weekly prayer in church." Why is it that at every level of society the Chrsitian faith is viewed as passé? Why are the lives of those "inside" not seen to be radically different from those "outside"? One answer: sin will always be with us and a part of us. But we are convinced of another answer, too: the lack of clear teaching from Scripture which applies faith in Christ and submission to His Lordship to every area of life.

About the Authors

The four people who cooperated in preparing this material are involved with the work of the Coalition for Christian Outreach. The Coalition is a cooperative effort of churches, colleges and universities in the tri-state area of northern West Virginia, eastern Ohio and western Pennsylvania. In its 13 years, the Coalition's staff members have grown from 4 to 150. The authors hold various positions in this ministry to students on forty-three campuses (about one-half of the campuses in the region).

Bradshaw L. Frey—Interim Director of Black Ministry, Brad coordinates the activities of a growing number of men and women who work with black college students. Undergraduate work at Geneva College preceeded his Master of Divinity and Master of Sacred Theology degrees from Pittsburgh Theological Seminary. He is currently a Ph.D. candidate in Foundations of Education at the University of Pittsburgh.

William E. Ingram—As Associate Director of Management Support Services, Bill focuses on the administrative support which the organization gives to the campus staff members and cooperating institutions. Following his college work at the University of Maryland, he received his Master of Divinity degree from Wesley Theological Seminary.

Thomas E. McWhertor—The Coalition's Director of Resource Development and Communications, Tom initiated the idea for this book and served as its Coordinator. His bachelor degree is from Grove City College, and he has a Master of Divinity degree from Gordon-Conwell Theological Seminary.

William David Romanowski—Bill is a professional musician and serves as a Resource Specialist with the Coalition. Performing in concerts, teaching college courses, and writing on contemporary issues and culture are all aspects of his ministry. Bill's undergraduate degree is from Indiana University of Pennsylvania, and he holds a masters degree in English from Youngstown State University.

Acknowledgements

This book is dedicated to our families:
Sue and Scott Frey,
Jeanette, Amy and Charlie Ingram,
Janice, Kata, Annie and Christopher McWhertor,
and Donna Romanowski (and Higgins!).

It is our hope that they, as well as the students who will lead our world in the near future, will be challenged to live Christian lives relevant to our culture, and that they may profit from our efforts to guide and teach.

We are grateful to a number of people who made significant contributions to this manuscript. We greatly appreciate the helpful reading and suggestions of Larry Edison, Marilyn Long, Gary Smith and Christy Wauzzinski, and the laborious typing and detail work of June Diehl, Helen Martin, and Cathie Miller. Also, we are grateful to Robert R. Long, Executive Director of the Coalition for Christian Outreach, for allotting us time and resources to develop the themes presented here.

Finally, we thank all those who have served as mentors in our lives. Since we each come from various backgrounds and educational experiences, we have had too many teachers to mention them all here; however, Dr. Peter J. Steen and Dr. Al Wolters stand out in relation to the contents of this volume. If anyone benefits from our efforts, these people deserve much credit. If there is culpability, it lies with the authors who spent eighteen enjoyable months strategizing and writing, hoping to convey the impact of the life, death, resurrection and ascension of Christ to men and women in the closing decades of the twentieth century.

May God be honored with our efforts.

Chapter 1

The Way Things Were

I was frustrated. Had I been so badly prepared? Would the whole course be so theoretical? I walked out of my first graduate sociology class with my head spinning. It seemed the professor spoke a foreign language. I sat on a bench between two huge concrete-and-glass buildings and tried to collect my thoughts. There, on the wall next to me, were lines of graffiti that struck home. In black magic marker some student had scrawled a cry for help. "I'm so confused it's beyond belief. I don't know what to believe anymore." How broken that person's experience. A class, a professor, a friend—something had thrown his or her whole life into confusion. No one was listening, and so the cry went out to anyone who would stop and read.

A young student's confusion and despair should be no surprise to us. Our culture is infected to its heart with this disease. Aren't we confused when people who claim to worship the same God kill each other? Don't we despair when people dress in hooded white costumes, burn crosses, and preach the superiority of white over black? I mourn my selfishness. I am discouraged by my lack of concern for other people. Racism, hunger, injustice, labor strikes, sexism, terrorism, pollution, rape—our world is fractured. Whether we are Christian or not, it is hard to avoid confusion and despair when we look at life honestly.

Normal or Abnormal

Even though "misery loves company," it is little consolation to know that we are not alone in our discouragement. To

1

know the confusion and despair of all of human history is no help. In fact, such knowledge pushes us to a disturbing question. Is this fractured life we experience normal? Is life supposed to be this way? With all of history as exhibit A, it seems the answer is yes. Throughout history people have resigned themselves to the belief that the brokenness of life is normal.

Many religions and philosophies have built this brokenness into their perception of reality. The ancient nature religions, which eventually influenced Greek philosophy, included human confusion and despair in the flow of life. For them this flow of life was a great river; all things emerged from it to take temporary existence and then eventually returned to the flow of the river. The flow of life was governed by mysterious forces or fate. No one ever explained the confusion and despair; it was simply a normal part of the life stream.[1]

"Eat, drink, and be merry, for tomorrow we die," is a phrase used to caricature the views of a later philosophical school, the Epicureans. Epicurus, a Greek philosopher who lived a few hundred years before Christ, did not himself seek sensual pleasure. He believed that mental bliss was the highest aim of man. He taught that the world was neither created nor governed by gods. Rather, it was formed by chance; death ends all, but it is not evil.[2] The devastation which brings life is normal. Not the problems of evil, but groundless fears of these problems are man's worst enemy. With this view of reality, it is understandable why his followers disavowed the meaning of life and sought to gratify sensual desires.

From Constantine (A.D. 326) until the Renaissance, which began in the fourteenth century, the Christian Church dominated western culture. During this time, many Christians agreed that confusion and despair were a normal part of this world. However, they lived in hope—a hope reserved for a future existence, an existence not in this world. From this perspective, physical life is by nature evil and destructive. One escapes physical life in order to go to heaven where spiritual life exists. The brokenness of our world simply has to be endured as long as one is in the body. Throughout the centuries, philosophic systems have not improved on these basic positions.

"Certainly," you say, "the three thousand years of human history that have elapsed since the time of nature religions have given us time to move beyond the concept that hurt, misery, suffering, and disintegration are normal!" But as the brokenness has persisted, so has the belief that the brokenness is normal. Martin Heidegger, one of the most significant philosophers of this century, argues that life is chaos. Having been "thrown" into existence, a person must realize that it is chaotic and meaningless. To be a true human being is to act as though life is meaningful, anyway. In the face of the anxiety which meaninglessness produces, a person can be "authentic" by refusing to despair, by living life to its fullest (maximizing human potential).[3] Many believe that this is a very courageous philosophy. But courageous or not, it still accepts the brokenness of this world as normal. It is just the way things are. We can confront the problems courageously or back away in cowardice, but the problems are simply a part of things. This perspective leads inevitably to a popularized form of fatalism: "There's no sense trying to change the bureaucracy." "Everyone knows that's the way those people are." "You only go 'round once, so you might as well grab for all the gusto you can get."

As Christians, shouldn't we oppose with all our might the view that brokenness is normal? I hope for a day when the brokenness is removed—not for a day when I have learned to live with it. The devastation around us is abnormal. We see its abnormality not when we look at history, but when we look toward God's intention and design.[4] As Christians, we look forward to a time when, "He will wipe every tear from their eyes. There will be no more death or mourning or crying or pain, for the old order of things has passed away" (Rev. 21:4). God the Creator is powerful. He is the loving Sustainer. His wisdom is unsearchable and His purposes cannot be frustrated. Brokenness violates God's loving intention. What would a world look like which was in harmony with God's personality and purposes?

Genesis 1 and 2

As Christians, we confess that God is just; yet our world is full of injustice. God is love, but hatred seems to permeate humankind. A well-known hymn begins, "Holy, Holy, Holy." So we honor God, but we who sing are profane. Any quality characteristic of God has its opposite quality in the reality of our world. John Lennon's song, "Imagine," asks us to think of a world without anguish and torment:

Imagine there's no countries
It isn't hard to do
Nothing to kill or die for
No religion too
Imagine all the people
Living life in peace . . .
Imagine no possessions
I wonder if you can
No need for greed or hunger
A brotherhood of man
Imagine all the people
Sharing all the world . . .

As Christians we do not affirm Lennon's outlook, but we share his desire to look beyond brokenness. Think of a world where all the perfect qualities of God find expression—a world where His power, love, wisdom, steadfastness, mercy, and beauty are in some way woven into the fabric of reality.

Do we have to strain our imaginations to picture such a world? Or are we wiser to accept Lennon's vague, surrealistic hope for the future? We do neither, for the first two chapters of Genesis give us a picture of the world in harmony with God. Christians who long for the healing of brokenness can find comfort in the beginning of the Bible. Christians who bitterly despise the devastation imposed on our world, may find help and encouragement to battle the forces which devastate all parts of our lives.

How does God express Himself in Genesis 1 and 2? What in these chapters shows how the world was responding to God? To understand this passage, we will examine it in three stages.[5] The first stage is creation out of nothing (ex nihilo).[6] There was nothing but God in the beginning. In His awesome power He calls the world into being. We may be "creative" as we form and rearrange things, but only God can call a world into being out of nothing. This first stage corresponds to Genesis 1:1, 2. God has made the basic "stuff" of creation. There was nothing, and then there was something.

Having made the basic "stuff" of creation, God proceeds in His formative work. The second stage of creation is diversification. Genesis 1:3 to 2:3 describes how God elaborates and enhances the creation. He separates light from darkness. He distinguishes dry land from the water. Plants and animals are called forth. Having shown His might and splendor in what He has created, God concludes the process by creating human beings. In His wisdom and love, God makes humans

the pinnacle of His creation by creating them in His own image. The immensity, diversity, and richness of the creation
give us some clues about the God who has made it all and
called it good.

Many people assume that here God finished His creative
work and turned the world over to human beings to see what
they would do with it. However, God's steadfastness means
that He never leaves or gives up on His creation. He remains
faithful constantly.

When we talk about a third stage of creation, it is with the
understanding that the God who acted in the first and second
stage keeps acting. In Genesis 1:28-30 and 2:15, we read about
the third stage of creation or the development of creation. In
the first two stages God Himself acted to accomplish His purpose, but in the third stage God chooses to accomplish His
purpose through humans. Men and women play a crucial role
at this point, but only as God gives them power.

In the third stage of creation, God enables humans to fill
and form the earth. In a sense God continues the second stage
of creation in the third stage, using human beings as His instruments. God places the creation in the care of people who
are to develop it. The potential God has created is to be re-
leased. The possibilities are to be explored. People are to pursue these responsibilities with honor and industry. According
to Genesis 1:28-30 people are to fill the earth, subdue it, and
rule over it. Genesis 2:15 also directs us to cultivate the earth.
These are serious tasks. Some of us grew up thinking that
Adam and Eve had nothing to do every day but run naked
through the garden and eat fruit. But God gave them great
responsibility. In fulfilling this responsibility, they found joy,
meaning and identity. It was no token job. They were to rule,
fill, subdue, and cultivate as they were empowered by God.
This was the third stage of creation.

Genesis 1 and 2 paint an exquisite picture of God's intention for the world. The crowning touch, however, comes in
Genesis 1:31. After completing the creation and setting human
beings at its zenith, God gazes at His work and says it is "very
good." It was not just "good" but "very good." Here He
declares that what He has made reflects who He is. He is glad
to take credit for what He has made.

It does not take a sage to look at our world and see that it
has very little in common with Genesis 1 and 2. Is Genesis
perhaps a fantasy story or has something altered our world
drastically? What made the normal so abnormal? Adam and
Eve could have lived in the garden for years and years joyfully

doing their tasks. But the devastation came quickly. Genesis 3 explains what so radically changed God's very good world.

God and Green Beans

A symbolic and fictional account may help us understand sin:

> One day, little Johnny walked into the kitchen to see what his mother was doing. "What'ya doin', Mom?" he said.
>
> "Just cooking some green beans for supper," she answered. "Now Johnny," she continued, "I have to go upstairs, and while I'm gone I don't want you to stick any of these green beans up your nose. If I find out that you have, I'll punish you," she said as she walked out of the kitchen.
>
> "That's ridiculous," thought Johnny, "who would want to stick green beans up his nose?" The more he thought about it, the more it made him wonder why his mother would even mention it. It was stupid. The thought even repulsed him.

To stick green beans up your nose is no more ridiculous than breaking any of God's laws. To go against the created order is ridiculous, for it violates God's intention. It is just as ridiculous to commit adultery as it is to try to breathe under water; the damage may not be as immediate, but the devastation is as thorough. It is ridiculous to violate the created order in any way.

> Johnny kept thinking about what his mother had said. "Ya know," he thought, "it would be kind of funny to see someone put green beans up his nose." He even had to chuckle as he pictured the scene in his mind. "Maybe I could get Mikey or Romo to do it. They'll do anything," he schemed.

There's something about disobedience: even to experience it vicariously can be satisfying.

> His amusement turned to resentment as he rehearsed the possibility. "Who does Mom think she is anyway? It's my nose isn't it? I'll stick green beans up it if I want to."
>
> He dragged a chair over to the stove, climbed onto it, and said, "I am the captain of my fate and master of my own destiny. I'll do whatever I want to do,

whenever I want." (He was a very well-read little boy.) With that, he took two medium-size diagonally cut green beans and headed for the dining room to perpetrate his disobedience.

Over the years many theologians have speculated about the nature of the first sin. Whatever its nature, it was certainly grounded in a strong strain of disbelief. Even though Adam and Eve were well aware that serious consequences would accompany disobedience, they refused to believe God when He told them what was good for them and that death would result from disobedience. Maybe it is not as much disbelief as misbelief. Johnny believed that his mother had no business ordering his life or reality. In the same way, humans refuse to acknowledge that the Creator and Sustainer of the world should determine right and wrong (not just morality). They will order reality for themselves; they believe that they are able to structure things themselves.

Disobedience always forces a person to hide from the person whose rule was broken. So it was with Johnny.

Afraid that his mother would return to the kitchen and find him, he tried to hide in a dark corner of the dining room, where he put the beans up his nose. Just then his mother happened to walk through the dining room and, seeing Johnny, she immediately realized what he had done.

"Johnny, I thought I told you *not* to put green beans up your nose," she snapped angrily. Trying to remain calm in this tense confrontation, he responded matter-of-factly, "Oh Mom, that wasn't me you told, that was my twin brother."

"You don't have a twin brother," came the reply.

"Well, I just said that because what really happened was so incredible. An elephant jumped out of the bread box and forced the green beans up my nose." Seeing that his mother was not accepting this story, he continued. "I have to confess, I was just trying to cover up for Mikey and Romo. They came in while you were gone and forced me to put them up my nose."

The result is inevitable: when we have chosen to rebel against reality as it is actually structured by God, we have to reconstruct reality so that we can live with it. Johnny couldn't simply acknowledge what he had done; he tried to change reality.[7]

The story of Johnny and the green beans introduces us to the devastating reality of sin. Sin is irrational; at its heart, sin is rebellion against God and refusal to acknowledge the truth of reality as He structured it. The only recourse is to try to structure reality according to one's own design.

Sin—this conscious rebellion against God and His order —is never partial. There is no such thing as moral neutrality. We either acknowledge God and His order or we attempt to create our own order. This absolute character of sin is always related to God and His will. David said, "Against you, you only, have I sinned and done what is evil in your sight . . ." (Ps. 51:4a). That doesn't mean our sin doesn't harm those around us or even the world in which we live, but precisely because it does and is in conflict with what God has directed, it is ultimately directed against God Himself. If I steal from my neighbor, I cause my neighbor to suffer, but ultimately my sin is an affront to God, who has told me to love my neighbor and not to steal from him.

Sin produces both guilt and pollution. Just as Johnny wanted to escape the presence of his mother, so our guilt drives us away from God. We are aware that we have willingly broken God's directives. We have no defense before God. Our changed relationship to God changes everything. Like Johnny, we try to structure reality in our own way. In this we see a principle of sin closely related to guilt—pollution. Pollution means that once sin enters a life it affects every part of it. No matter what aspect of a person's being you consider, you can be sure sin has had a terrible impact on it. A person cannot act without somehow expressing sin.

Jesus made it clear in the fifth chapter of Matthew that sin is more than outward acts. He condemned hatred and lust as sharply as murder and adultery. Sin is irrational *rebellion*. Sin is an absolute *lie*. Sin is *against God;* it is pollution. It is inward as well as outward. Sin grips the issues of life; all of our lives are broken and twisted by sin's all-*encompassing* grip.[8]

I remember vividly one day when a professor told a seminary class that each one of us, because of the power of sin, could be another Adolf Hitler. The potential of our wickedness was without limit. You could have heard a pin drop; each student knew that the professor was right. It was much like the disciples hearing Jesus say that one of them would betray Him. There was no finger pointing because each one knew he was capable of such a hideous deed. One by one, they asked, "Is it I?"

Three Stages of Sin

I wish I could stop here with the description of sin. Even as I continue, I realize that the fullest description I could give would not convey sin's awful reality. So far, we have looked at the impact of sin on individuals. But the effects of sin extend far beyond individual lives. To see the scope of that impact, recall the three stages of creation (pp. 4-5).

As we have seen, God creates in three levels or stages. In the first He creates the basic "stuff" of creation; in the second, He diversifies and elaborates a rich, full world; and in the third, He empowers people as His instruments to continue to develop the potential He created. Humans were to have dominion and cultivate. They would, for example, develop agriculture as they cultivated the earth. With specialization and further differentiation, they would have developed some system of trade to exchange their different foods, and so on.

Once humans determine that they will structure reality in opposition to God, sin also moves through the stages of creation. Now we have stages of creation polluted, last to first, by sin. Humans were given dominion over the world to develop it. Since in their rebellion against God, they reject His design, they live outside His plan and protection—in sin. As they unlock the potential of the creation in a perverted way, agriculture and then the system of trade which followed turned out to be sinful rather than good. Because the people who developed creation by forming culture were polluted, sin became deeply embedded in culture.

We must remember that the three stages of creation are one created order which goes through three stages of development. Therefore, when sin infects the creation at the third stage it works back through stages two and one to affect the very "stuff" of creation. In Genesis 3:17-18, for example, the very ground is cursed because of Adam's sin. No longer will the ground produce only good grain; now it will also produce thistles. That is why in Romans 8:22 Paul says, ". . . the whole creation has been groaning as in the pains of childbirth." We may think at once of how we have polluted air and water, but we should recognize, too, the breakdown of the family and corruption in government as perversions of God's order.

The scope of sin is enormous. It touches every aspect of individual life and every part of creation. Thoughts, physical things, actions, individuals, and institutions are all unable to escape sin's influence. Its infection is total. Its extent is limitless.

The World and the Flesh

Seeing the full catastrophe of sin leads some people to despair. The everyday power of sin often beats people down. It is understandable, then, that people identify the devastation of sin with the New Testament concepts of world and flesh. Both concepts are used to speak of a world order in total conflict with the rule of Christ. Examples are I John 2:15a, where John says, "Do not love the world or anything in the world;" and Ephesians 2:3a, where Paul says, "All of us also lived among them at one time, gratifying the cravings of our sinful nature (or "flesh") and following its desires and thoughts." Both world and flesh denote human life as it has been ravaged by sin. Both words are negative; they refer to something which is to be avoided.[8]

These verses are clear, but Christians can jump from them to hasty, false conclusions. Are "the world" and "the flesh" evil? We know that the effect of sin extends to all parts of the creation. It is also clear that "the world" and "the flesh" includes everything physical. However, a brief analysis of the New Testament will show us there is more to the discussion.

World and flesh are not always used in a negative sense in the New Testament. Both words are sometimes used in a descriptive or neutral way. In Acts 17:6 Jason and some others are dragged before city officials and the charge made is, "These men who have caused trouble all over the world have now come here . . ." Here, "world" is simply a geographic description. In Ephesians 6:12, Paul writes, "For our struggle is not against flesh and blood, but against the rulers, against the authorities, against the powers of this dark world and against the spiritual forces of evil in the heavenly realms." Here also, flesh seems to be just a biological description of humanity.

In fact, world and flesh are both used in a positive way in the New Testament. In the well-known verse, John 3:16, John writes, "For God so loved the world . . ." If "world" meant only that physical reality infected and dominated by sin, it could hardly be the object of God's unqualified love. In the same way, John in his gospel writes, in 1:14, "The Word became flesh . . ." If flesh were totally corrupt and at all points to be despised, it seems unlikely that the perfect Lord of the universe would choose to inhabit such a form.

This leaves us with two questions. The first: Do Bible writers contradict themselves and each other as they use these words? The second question concerns the positive use of "world" and "flesh." If we can speak of those entities in some positive way, can the destructive effects of sin be as complete as we said earlier? There is a way out of the dilemma posed by these questions. The answer does more than solve our uncomfortable tension; it provides us with a basis for hope.

Perversion not Destruction

Tension arises from the fact that both world and flesh have positive and negative meanings. But rather than contradicting each other, the Bible writers seem to be using these words in different ways. The letter of John which tells us not to love the world does not contradict the Gospel of John, where God does in fact love the world enough to send His Son to die for it. When John's first letter tells us not to love the world, he is speaking of the world as the totality of sin-infected creation.[9] It is the sum of that which sin has distorted and perverted. The world we are not to love is the world which hates God and seeks to establish its own order of reality. A similar and parallel argument could be made for the word "flesh."[10] When in the Gospel, John says that God loves the world, he means that God loves the created order. He loves His plan for creation. God loves the basic structure of the world, the world as He made it.

When sin entered the world, its effect was to pervert Creation, not to destroy it. This perversion was thorough and encompassed every aspect of creation, but God did not let the very structure or order of creation tumble. Sin is an alien invasion. It is parasitic. Sin can live off the creation, but it cannot replace it. An example of this principle can be seen in two institutions which were introduced before the Fall: marriage and family. According to Genesis 2, it is not good for man to be alone, and so woman is created and they come together in marriage. In Genesis 1 we are told to fill the earth—a command for family. But soon after the Fall we see both marriage and family distorted. There will be unfaithfulness in marriage, and brother killing brother as family breaks down. God commands the institutions of marriage and family, and He hates how sinful human beings pervert them. Today, with unfaithfulness in marriage, divorce, and the "gay movement" rising, some say that family and marriage are doomed. But family and marriage were created by God and pronounced good. And though God hates the perversion of those struc- tures, He still loves the structures themselves. Because family and marriage are built into the structure of creation, they will always continue. That is why it is not surprising that most divorced people remarry. It should also not surprise us to hear of "gay" marriages and "gay" couples trying to adopt children. God's creation order holds no matter how we pervert it.

God loves the world which He created, diversified, and elaborated. He continues to love the structure of the world which remains. But God hates what humans have done with it. He hates what sinful stewards have made of His creation. He hates our wickedness, our injustice, and our rebellion. He hates the way our perversion has blighted all levels and aspects of His world.

It is a sad picture, but it is not hopeless. Our hope is twofold. First, it is built on our knowledge that God is the sovereign Creator of the universe. Though sin has invaded His creation, we know that God can overcome it. Second, our hope is built on our knowledge that there is still a basic structure or order to our world that has not been destroyed by sin. We know that God is a faithful God and that He has called the world into existence for a good purpose. God will restore His original intention. We know that He can . . . we know that He will.

Notes

1. Gordon H. Clark, *Thales to Dewey: A History of Philosophy* (Boston: Houghton Mifflin Company, 1957), pp. 17-19.
2. Williston Walker, *A History of the Christian Church* (New York: Charles Scribner's Sons, 1918), p. 6.
3. R.C. Sproul, *The Symbol: An Exposition of the Apostles' Creed* (Philadelphia: The Presbyterian and Reformed Publishing Company, 1973), p. 27.
4. Abraham Kuyper, *Lectures on Calvinism* (Grand Rapids: William B. Eerdmans Publishing Company, 1931), p. 132.
5. Albert Wolters, "Encountering the Secular Mind," Coali- tion for Christian Outreach Spring Training, Grove City, PA, May, 1980. We are also indebted to Dr. Wolters for stimulating thoughts which have led to the development of other parts of this chapter. Also, in examining various

alternatives to creation, we have found Francis Schaeffer's book, *Genesis in Space and Time* (IVP), a helpful starting point.

6. The language of Genesis 1 is not the clearest biblical source of this. Hebrews 11:3 is an illustration of a more definitive statement of this truth.

7. The "Green Bean Analogy" was conceived and popularized by David Terry Thomas, a well-known speaker in the greater Pittsburgh area.

8. For a more elaborate discussion of the nature of sin the reader should see Louis Berkhof's, *Systematic Theology* (William B. Eerdmans Publishing Company).

9. Albert Wolters, "Encountering the Secular Mind."

10. For further study of these words see Richard Mouw's, *Called to Holy Worldliness* (Fortress) and *The New Bible Dictionary* (IVP), J.D. Douglas, ed.

Chapter 2

God So Loved the World

T he good news of the Bible is the news that God has acted. His love is so great for His creation that the moment human beings acted to separate the creation from its source, God acted to restore the relationship. God so loved the world (see pp. 3-5) that He gave His Son for it (John 3:16). This is the strongest possible affirmation that He has not given up on the creation. The story of the Old and New Testaments is that God will not allow satan and those who choose to follow him to be victorious. God has called creation into being by His powerful Word, and He brings what He has created back to Himself.

A Foundation for Hope

People stood in the doorways of the ballroom crowded to capacity. Upon the intense silence of the room fell the words of Dr. Anthony Campolo, retelling a black preacher's masterful sermon: "It's Friday but Sunday's comin' "—five simple but powerful words. As Campolo developed the idea, he kept repeating the refrain. Only whispering it at first, he came back again and again to that simple phrase, leading the crowd toward hope. Finally, as the sermon rose to a crescendo, he screamed, "It's Fri-i-day!" Three thousand people rose to their feet and shouted in a joyful response: "But Sunday's comin'!" The room was flooded with applause and whistling, screaming and laughter, tears and people embracing one another during this dramatic encounter with Christian hope.

The stunning power of "It's Friday—but Sunday's comin'!" is that this phrase captures the essence of Christian hope. "Friday" (the crucifixion) is a symbol of the devastation that sin has wrought on the good creation of God. "Sunday's comin' " (the resurrection) is a symbol of our faithful God and His unwillingness to allow sin to have the final say. The phrase explodes with hope when we see how God acts to redeem what He created.

God responded in an amazing way to Adam's rebellion. In the first two chapters of Genesis, we see the beautiful creation God made. In the third chapter we see the creation devastated by sin. But before the end of the chapter God is at work to buy back His creation. If Dr. Campolo's talk brings hope, think of the unbounded optimism that Genesis 3:15 can give us. This verse is the foundation for all the hope which echoes throughout the Bible. Speaking to the serpent, God says, "I will put enmity between you and the woman, and between your offspring and hers; he will crush your head and you will strike his heel" (Gen. 3:15). The promise embodies three dimensions of hope. First, there will be a future. Imagine what a comfort that would have been for Adam and Eve, who didn't know how severe God's punishment would be. A future means hope. For ancient people, the idea of children and descendants (offspring) was a concrete way to think about that future. The promise of a role for their offspring was an affirmation of the future.

Second, the battle motif of this verse gives us hope. Humans will be able to confront the Prince of Darkness throughout the course of history. Genesis 3:15 prefigures history as a conflict between the "father of lies" and the champion of God. The followers of darkness will cling desperately to their power and imagined victory while those who follow the rightful King are busy reclaiming the creation in His name. We are participants in this battle which is fought upon the panorama of history.

The third and climactic element of hope in this verse is the promise that the devastating presence and power of darkness will finally be obliterated. "He (the offspring of the woman) will crush your head," is God's way, in promise form, of saying that He will one day remove the effects of sin from His creation. The hope for redemption is centered in the offspring of the woman. The long wait for this offspring marks the mood of the Old Testament, as God unfolds the history of redemption.

A Mediator Fails

Throughout the Old Testament, we wait to see what the personification of the hope promised in Genesis 3:15 will look like. What will be his qualities and identity? Various themes shed light on these questions. The Levitical sacrifices suggest that our hope rests in a sacrifice which God will provide. The good kings of Israel typify that the "offspring" will be a King of kings. The hope of the nations is not only to look to the light of Israel but to expect that someday ambassadors of the "new Israel" will arrive. The prophets anticipated a time when the "offspring" would become the Word of God in flesh dwelling among us. These themes and others point toward a mediator, one who would stand between God and His people. He would be the sacrifice; He would reign as King of kings, send ambassadors to the ends of the earth, and embody the word of God, thereby fulfilling our promised hope.

In the Old Testament, we see many different mediators, various leaders who stand between God and His people. Moses is perhaps the person who best illustrates what the promised Mediator would be like. He was most conscious of his role as mediator between God and His people. And his role as a mediator had a variety of aspects. Moses would enter the "tent of meeting" to represent the needs and desires of the people of Israel in the presence of God and then emerge with His directives for the people (Ex. 33:7ff). Moses had mediated for the Israelites with Pharaoh and secured their release. This mediation eventually opened up new possibilities for their work, families and worship. And finally, Moses was the mediator of the Law. Not only did God liberate His people, He also gave a description of what liberated life should look like. The Law which Moses mediated covered every phase of life: trade and commerce, agriculture, rites and rituals, justice between people, family and marriage, education, and personal hygiene. Even land and animals are included.[1]

Moses was also a central figure in the life of Israel. The well-being of his people seemed to rest on his shoulders. A certain cycle seemed to develop over time. Moses would declare the will of the Lord for His people. The people, after a time of obedience, would stray away from God's intentions. Then they would be chastised. Moses would plead with God for mercy and then call the people back to God's ordinances. This pattern repeats itself several times until it climaxes in Numbers 11.

Once the Israelites had feared starvation in the wilderness, but God had graciously met their need by providing manna. Numbers 11 tells us that "manna was like coriander seed and looked like resin." To prepare it, the people would grind it or crush it and either cook it in a pot or make cakes. However, even the most resourceful Israelite could only find so many ways to cook manna. There was fried manna, baked manna, boiled manna, poached manna, manna soufle, manna flambe, manna for breakfast, manna for lunch, manna for dinner, manna, manna, manna. By now the Israelites had forgotten their deliverance from Egypt and from starvation. They could think only of their bland diet. In their self-pity they wailed, "Give us an onion, or a garlic or a leek, anything for a little flavor" or they moaned, "We need cucumbers or melons, something for variety." But most of all they cried for meat to eat. They began to long for life as it had been in Egypt. Time and again, Moses had confronted the Israelites, struggling to try to persuade them to return to the Lord—until now. He had brought them out of Egypt, given them the Law and even gone before the Lord with their concerns. This, indeed, was the "straw which broke the camel's back." Under more pressure and tension than any one human being could stand, Moses broke down. Crushed by the load he carried, he renounced his position as mediator. The once courageous leader crumbled to pieces: "Why, God, did you do this to me?" Feeling the role of mediator not as joy but as punishment, he cried out, "What have I done to displease you, that you put the burden of all these people on me?" Moses wanted out. He concluded his bitter lament with the plea, "If this is how you are going to treat me put me to death right now." Moses said to God, "I'd rather you kill me than make me continue as the mediator." And yet Moses was one of the most heroic figures of the Old Testament—one of the most courageous, strong, and moral people of human history. Moses is one of the best that humanity could offer and yet he was crushed by the role of mediator.

The weight of trying to mediate between God and His people crushed Moses and would certainly crush any of us had we been in his place. God Himself would have to provide One who could bear the burden, and He did. The night before His crucifixion Christ knelt in the Garden of Gethsemane to pray, and He realized that His calling was to be the mediator Moses failed to be (Luke 22:39-46). God showed Him the weight of what He had to carry and the suffering which would accompany it. Jesus was not surprised; he was not swept along by

events. That night God showed Jesus exactly what it would
mean to be the mediator.[2] Lest we think the burden had
become lighter over the years, the Bible tells us that faced
with His awesome task, Jesus Christ was in anguish and, "he
prayed more earnestly, and his sweat was like drops of blood
falling on the ground." This rare physical condition is pro-
duced only under extreme stress and anxiety. The weight of
mediating between God and His people had become no
lighter. However, Jesus was able to carry the weight that
crushed Moses. Moses would rather be put to death than be
the mediator, while Jesus was willing to be put to death to be
the mediator. What the man Moses couldn't do, the God-man
Jesus could. Anguish, heartbreak and turmoil would come to
Him, but His confession, "not my will, but yours be done," is
the grand affirmation that in Jesus we have the mediator at
last.

Moses brought freedom and the possibility for new life to
the Israelites. He brought them the law which explained the
dimensions of that new life. He stood before God on behalf of
his people in the tent of meeting. However, Moses only
foreshadowed and pointed to the One who would adequately
stand between God and His people. The possibilities Moses
opened up for all of life find their full expression in the Christ
who came that we might have life and have it abundantly
(John 10:10).

Christ the Mediator

Moses served as the prophet of the Lord, delivering the
Law from Sinai and speaking the Word of God to His covenant
people. He served as priest, establishing the Levitical
priesthood to plead man's case with God. He served as king,
leading the nation out of Egypt to the edge of the land of
promise. However, his performance in these roles gave only a
taste of the true Prophet, Priest and King—Christ Jesus.

As Prophet, Jesus was the Word of God incarnate. His
words were God's words! Moses, Elijah, Isaiah and other prophets were called to reveal the will of God to the people. As
they were instructed, so they instructed the people of God.
Christ revealed the will of God in His person. He speaks of
Himself as prophet (Luke 13:33); He speaks with the authority
of God (Matt. 7:29). The Old Testament prophets can be compared to emissaries sent by a national leader. They speak with
authority but not nearly the authority of the King's Son. The
Son of God, Christ, is the greatest prophet.

As Priest, Jesus fulfilled what the role of priest in the Old Testament only approximated. On behalf of the people, the priests pleaded for the gracious mercy of God. The sacrificial system was established as a means of forgiveness. Christ, as Priest, is the fulfillment of all that the priests before Him anticipated. Christ pleads the cause of believers with the Father (I John 2:1), against satan, the accuser. His death alone offers the perfect sacrifice for sin—the sacrifice of His perfect life. The Hebrew priests saw how completely sinful man was separated from God, for they saw the distance between holiness and sin. Christ bridged the gulf by becoming man and suffering all the temptations of humanity, yet without sin. He, and He alone, was able to offer the perfect sacrifice for the sins of a fallen world. Christ gave His own life willingly for the lives of His people, just as a father may willingly risk his life—and lose it, to save the life of his child.

As King, Jesus fulfilled the ultimate kingship only glimpsed in the Old Testament office of king. Moses' leadership role anticipated the appointment of Saul as King of Israel, followed by David and Solomon. But these rulers governed merely geographical kingdoms and their lives were marked by the shortcomings chronicled in Scripture. Christ is the King of all; He is given the power to rule over all things in heaven and on earth (Col. 1:15ff). He not only rules over the church, His people, He also sovereignly administrates the universe.

As Priest, Christ has given His blood to restore humanity's relationship with God. He is the perfect sacrifice.[3] As Prophet, Christ speaks the will of God to believers so that they may bring their lives into conformity with the righteousness that is declared because of His sacrifice. As King, Christ gives the assurance and security that God reigns. In the role of Christ as Mediator, all the promises given by God are fulfilled and God's people (that's us!) are restored to their proper place as redeemed servants of the King.

Christ the Mediator is the second Adam, the one who does all that Adam was supposed to do and more. When Adam and Eve failed to obey the will of God, their disobedience plunged creation into sin and death. Jesus became human so that in His life He might fulfill the command of obedience given to Adam and that in His death "He might destroy him who holds the power of death . . . and free those who all their lives were held in slavery . . ." He has made atonement for sin, once for all (Heb. 2:14-18). Christ perfectly obeyed the will of God in every way. His perfect life was a sacrifice which could redeem a fallen humanity. But Christ not only died for Adam's sin, He did what Adam failed to do—obey the will of God. His shed blood and His obedience reversed the direction of the fallen world. Adam's sin set corruption in motion. Humanity's sinful efforts to cultivate the creation actually distorted it; humanity perverted what God had made good. For example, instead of seeing God's norms for marriage as guidelines for love in its fullest sense, humanity has viewed the institution as demanding, restrictive and oppressive. Instead of embracing the good institution God gave, humanity has twisted and abused it—but not beyond recognition. Instead of seeing "justice" as a God-given norm for life, humanity has perverted the idea to an oppressive one. Rulers view "justice" as the undermining of their authority; the downtrodden see "justice" as a tool of those who oppress them. Yet both seek "justice" because it belongs to created reality, even though it is continually twisted by a fallen world. What God made has been perverted by sin, but is still recognizable, if only barely.

Christ, the second Adam, reversed this direction. Redeemed men, women, and children live their lives in obedience through the example and power of the second Adam—not the first.

Just as the first Adam was the head of the fallen world, the second Adam is the head of a redeemed world. His perfect life and sacrificial death are the basis of a new orientation for all creation. The scope of deliverance in Christ is magnificent —redemption is as wide as creation itself.

Amazing Grace

Nearly every believer has sung about God's amazing grace—"I once was blind, but now I see." When Jesus' disciples asked Him why He spoke in parables, He answered:

> The knowledge of the secrets of the kingdom of heaven has been given to you, but not to them. Whoever has will be given more, and he will have an abundance. Whoever does not have, even what he has will be taken from him. This is why I speak in parables, though seeing, they do not see; though hearing, they do not hear or understand. But blessed are your eyes because they see, and your ears because they hear (Matt. 13:11-13).

A redeemed citizen of God's Kingdom has eyes to see and ears to hear. But what does that mean? It means that God has given us a vision for the true meaning of things. Redeemed people know that there is more to life and the world than what we experience with the five senses. The way we "see" and understand things, or interpret events is colored by what we believe about life in general. Everyone has a "map" of reality which defines the meaning and purpose of life.

The most obvious mark of a Christian picture of the universe (cosmos) is that it depends on the existence of God. God does exist; He is there, and not as a cosmic killjoy whose rules for life are oppressive and burdensome. Neither is He an uninterested clockmaker who created the world and stands by while it runs its course. God is not a vindictive fate who plays with people like pieces on a chessboard, nor is He the forgetful dreamer whose fleeting thoughts comprise the universe. God is a loving and personal God intimately involved with His creation. He reveals Himself and the Truth about life through His work in creation and in Scripture. God has demonstrated throughout history that He is always faithful to what He has made and that His love and patience extend as far as the death of His own Son for the redemption of His handiwork.

If we know who God is, we begin to understand who humans are and what they are doing in the world. We are not an animal species which has risen to dominance because of our ability to reason, or to make tools, or to use metaphors. Rather, humans are creatures created by God in His own image as the crown of creation. The whole human being, male and female alike, at work or play, in his or her body, soul, mind, and emotions, reflects our Maker. Humans have fallen, but they can be forgiven and redeemed in Christ. Redeemed human creatures are restored to their proper place in their Father's world as stewards, entrusted by God with the task of cultivating and caring for His creation. Thus, they take on God-given authority, responsibility and service; this is the essence of their lives in the created world.

"Seeing" humans in this perspective allows us to hope for a genuine human community of love, compassion and communication. All of us are fallen creatures in the dwelling place God created for us. Our task is to work together serving one another for God's sake, making the world a place which demonstrates His wisdom and glory. We are not autonomous individuals who must learn to swim or sink for ourselves. We do not have an inherent goodness and dignity which will lead us with confidence to our own self-made perfection. Through our redemption to new life in Christ Jesus, we are restored to our proper place of responsibility to God and to our neighbor whom we must love as ourselves.

As a community of "neighbors," our task is to care for and cultivate the reality God formed. The universe is not a self-existent "Nature," hostile to humans, but the realm in which we are to exercise our God-given task of dominion. Though the effects of sin make life seem fragmented and even absurd, the eyes of faith can see the meaning and unity of things in God's creation, which even in its fallen state is now being redeemed by Christ and remains our Father's world. Gordon J. Spykman explains:

> In the original order of things, there was no room for segregation from God, or from our fellow men, or from the world. God the great worker also commissioned man to be his understudy and co-worker, cultivating the earth, naming the animals, populating this globe—which translated into modern parlance, means agriculture and industry, science and art, technology and research, music and literature, homemaking and schoolwork, and a hundred and one other tasks. This is our cultural mandate.[4]

All of us have experienced relationship with God, ourselves, others, and the world. But to see them as a unity, as one integrated whole picture of a Christian's place in the cosmos, helps us to understand the meaning of redemption in Christ for our daily lives. Because we believe in the existence of both the visible and the invisible, we Christians approach the affairs of everyday life in a different way than unbelievers do. There is a different understanding of the matters of life for those whose eyes have been opened by the grace of God. For example, Elisha's servant was filled with fear when he rose early in the morning and saw the city surrounded by the Syrian army with horses and chariots. But his fear was relieved when the Lord opened his eyes to "see" that there was a host of angels with fiery chariots and horses surrounding Elisha, a host that outnumbered the Syrian army (II Kings 6:8-23). Believers whose eyes are redeemed by God's amazing grace can "see" what people do not ordinarily see. And yet, it is the ordinary that takes on new meaning.

Without this new gift of sight, death seems to be the end of things; we should indeed "grab for all the gusto you can get." If we are not responsible to God, we should make our short lives as enjoyable as possible. Central air conditioning and a second color television will be more important than a contribution to help starving people in some far-away corner of the globe. We will continue to save pennies at the supermarket rather than support a boycott which might help improve working conditions for farmworkers. It is more advantageous to have the boss and his wife over for dinner than the widow and her children who live at the end of the street. Bars on your store window and a new burglar alarm system might not build trust within your community, but they will lower your insurance rates.

Consider these matters as one whose life has been redeemed by Christ:

> "Come, you who are blessed by my Father; take your inheritance, the kingdom prepared for you since the creation of the world. For I was hungry and you gave me something to eat, I was thirsty and you gave me something to drink, I was a stranger and you invited me in, I needed clothes and you clothed me, I was sick and you looked after me, I was in prison and you came to visit me . . . I tell you the truth, whatever you did for one of the least of these brothers of mine, you did for me" (Matt. 25:34-36, 40b).

What looks like foolishness to an unbeliever is right and good in the eyes of faith. Our Father in heaven reveals to us His vision for His creation. Redeemed people can discern when something is right or wrong according to God's intentions; they have ears to listen to God's Word for direction in the affairs of life, and, empowered by the Holy Spirit, they take responsibility for obedience. All of this means that they understand daily life in the context of God's care for His creation.

Our Christian picture of the cosmos reveals fallen people in a fallen world with only one hope: that the whole creation will be redeemed by the blood of the Creator's Son. The apostle Paul tells us:

> We know that the whole creation has been groaning as in the pains of childbirth right up to the present time. Not only so, but we ourselves, who have the firstfruits of the Spirit, groan inwardly as we wait eagerly for our adoption as sons, the redemption of our bodies. For in this hope we were saved. But hope that is seen is no hope at all. Who hopes for what he already has? But if we hope for what we do not yet have, we wait for it patiently (Rom. 8:22-25).

We color in our picture of the cosmos with the knowledge that "in all things God works for the good of those who love him, who have been called according to his purpose." In everything "we are more than conquerors through him who loved us." The apostle Paul, recognizing the power available through the redemption of Christ, says in his letter to the Ephesians:

> I pray also that the eyes of your heart may be en-
> lightened in order that you may know the hope to
> which he has called you, the riches of his glorious
> inheritance in the saints, and his incomparably great
> power for us who believe. That power is like the
> working of his mighty strength, which he exerted in
> Christ when he raised him from the dead and seated
> him at his right hand in the heavenly realms, far
> above all rule and authority, power and dominion,
> and every title that can be given, not only in the
> present age but also in the one to come. And God
> placed all things under his feet and appointed him to
> be head over everything for the church, which is his
> body, the fullness of him who fills everything in every
> way (Eph. 1:18-23).

The fulfillment of our redemption by Christ is the restoration of all things to their proper place—under the Lordship of Christ. Our hope is for what we do not yet see—the complete renewal of God's creation.

Notes

1. Hendrik Hart, *Will All the King's Men . . .: Out of Concern for the Church, Phase II* (Toronto: Wedge Publishing Foundation, 1972), p. 34.
2. S.G. DeGraaff, *Promise and Deliverance; Volume I: From Creation to the Conquest of Canaan* (St. Catharines, Ontario: Paideia Press, 1977), pp. 10-30.
3. For a systematic and theological treatment of the doctrine of the atonement, cite the following:
    L. Berkhof, *Systematic Theology* (Grand Rapids, MI: William B. Eerdmans Publishing Company, 1939, 1941), pp. 367-399.
    G.C. Berkouwer, *The Work of Christ* (Grand Rapids, MI: William B. Eerdmans Publishing Company, 1965).
    Charles Hodge, *Systematic Theology* (Grand Rapids,

MI: William B. Eerdmans Publishing Company, reprinted 1972).

John Murray, *Redemption Accomplished and Applied* (Grand Rapids, MI: William B. Eerdmans Publishing Company, 1955).

Roger Nicole, "The Nature of Redemption," in *Christian Faith and Modern Theology*, Carl F.H. Henry, ed. (New York: Channel Press, 1964), pp. 193-222.

John Owen, D.D., *The Death of Death in the Death of Christ* (London: The Banner of Truth Trust, reprinted 1959 with introductory essay by J.I. Packer).

J.I. Packer, "What Did the Cross Achieve?: The Logic of Penal Substitution," *Tyndale Bulletin*, 25, 1974, pp. 3-45.

Benjamin Breckinridge Warfield, *The Person and Work of Christ*, Samuel G. Craig, ed. (Philadelphia: The Presbyterian and Reformed Publishing Company, 1950).

4. Gordon J. Spykman, *Christian Faith in Focus* (Grand Rapids, MI: Baker Book House, 1967), p. 49.

Chapter 3

Redemption Results in Restoration

Redemption in Christ is God's gracious response to a fallen creation. Redemption, understood in its fullness, gives meaning to everyday life.

The richness of biblical language and biblical imagery should help us to see this everyday meaning. However, the theological and historical realities of our redemption have not been communicated very well to successive generations of Christians. Now it is often the case that communities of believers live without understanding how their redemption has an impact on moment-by-moment living. The course of their normal activities fails to demonstrate the health and wholeness of life in Christ.

Somehow we must gain new insights into the meaning of our redemption, or the benefits we ignore will be lost until Christ returns to establish His Kingdom in all of its fullness. We must make redemption understandable to the world around us. We must give the biblical imagery contemporary meaning.

The kind of events which the Bible reports would seem bizarre if they appeared on the pages of our daily papers. The fictional story which follows is an attempt to explain restoration to modern man in modern terms. Though we do experience restoration in our daily lives, it still seems unbelievable to us. This example shows how restoration means recovering what was lost and more.

Once There Was a Man
Who Was a University President . . .

Hundreds of students crowded together on the university lawn, a collage of spring colors on the green grass. Hand-painted signs bobbed on the sea of protesters as they marched and chanted and filled the air with songs and bull-horn speeches. "This university is an asylum!" a student leader shouted. "It's a sanctuary!"

"Yeah! Yeah!" the crowd responded.

"We've been disconnected from what's really happening in the world. And politics is at the heart of the issue!"

"All right! All right!"

"Nothing's going to change the political direction of this country, or this state, or this university unless we begin here and unite to stand up to the administration!"

Their cheers and whistles could not be heard on the top floor of the administration building. At least not while the temperature-control unit was running. President Kendrick was speaking. "One of the basic purposes of higher education is the preservation, transmission, and enrichment of the important elements of culture through research, scholarship, creative imagination and human experience. It is the task of this university to vitalize this and other educational purposes so as to assist the student in developing his or her potential to the limit and making his or her contribution to the betterment of society."

The members of the board applauded as President Kendrick concluded his speech and returned to his seat. Mr. Thomas Forbes, the Chairman of the Board, took his place at the podium and concluded the program. "Thank you, Dr. Kendrick, for a most encouraging account of the state of affairs here at our university. Ladies and Gentlemen, coffee is being served in the outer room."

While mingling with the board members, Dr. Kendrick was greeted by John Delvin who shook his hand and said, "Michael, that was a splendid presentation. It sounds like things are moving along just fine. How are Ann and the kids?"

"They're doing well, John," he replied. "Ann's mother, though, is sick again and needs a lot of attention, so it's convenient living so close to her. She and Ann have always been close, especially since Ann's father died."

"Well, tell them I send my love and hope Ann's mother is feeling better."

"I will."

"By the way, Mike, have you caught up with Brad Winston?"

"I appreciate your giving me that contact."

"Well, he expressed some interest in investing in higher education. How did it go with him?"

"I got a letter off to him, but I haven't been able to meet with him yet. There's a bit of student unrest over this Mideast thing and it's taking some time trying to keep a lid on it."

"Don't wait too long to contact him. You can't continue to rely so heavily on state funding. It's your primary responsibility to develop private-sector contacts, along with the governmental ones. You're younger than most university presidents and don't have as large a field of experience to draw from yet. I knew that when we moved you into this position, and it's going to take some time and work."

"I realize that," Kendrick replied. "I appreciate your help, John. Not to change the subject, but the word I hear is that you're resigning from the board. Is that true?"

"Well, serving on the boards of two universities can cut into your time. And in fact, I'll be serving as the new chairman of the board of State University."

"Well, congratulations, John!"

"Oh, it's not official yet, but it will be in a month or two."

"That's great news. Great news."

The next morning Kendrick entered his office and asked his secretary if there were any messages.

"A group of students submitted a petition. They'd like a meeting with you to discuss raising the political consciousness of the university," she said with a grin. *"Oh, and a Mr. Winston phoned."*

"Thanks, Jane," he said as he stepped into his office, closing the door behind him. Choosing to ignore the messages, he spent the rest of the morning working on the budget for the next school year, signing the papers allocating funds for a new project in scientific research, and finalizing details concerning the speaker for graduation.

That spring, there was a small student demonstration at graduation. But Kendrick left all university problems behind while he vacationed with his family at the shore. His freedom was short-lived, though; Ann's mother was hospitalized after suffering another heart attack and the family returned to be with her.

Kendrick's desk at the university was covered with letters and telephone messages when he returned. Among them was a *letter from the State Educational Department: ". . . As a result of the crisis in the Mideast, revenue from local oil refineries will be severely reduced and, accordingly, our State governmental expenditures must be reappropriated. Hence, our previously proposed allocation to your institution will be decreased by 45 percent . . ."*

Kendrick was on the telephone immediately to the State Capitol. *"Bill, isn't this cut a bit unrealistic? I mean, how are we going to survive? Were the other State schools cut so drastically?"*

"Mike,"—*there was a pause in his reply. "Off the record, I think those student demonstrations at your campus ruffled some feathers down here and moved some legislators to treat you a little less kindly when the heat was turned up. I'm sorry."*

There was a long moment of silence while the administrator stood gazing out his large window at the spacious campus below where students strolled along the paths between buildings. It suddenly seemed to him to be a life-sized map of reality. The social science hall was linked to the business building by an enclosed bridge; a long winding path led to the recreational center, with arteries extending to the theatre, the English building, and the fine arts studios. Behind them the student union was nestled among residence halls surrounded by tennis and basketball courts. Below him, a walkway led to the political science building, but he couldn't see that building. Standing at the heart of the institution, he wrestled with himself: *How could he keep it alive and well?*

The intercom buzzed; Jane informed him that Mr. Thomas Forbes was calling. Their conversation was long and stilted. Had he anticipated the political situation? Were funds available in the private sector? What did he propose to do? Had he developed the necessary contacts to raise the funds for the current budget? Forbes strongly intimated that Kendrick's answers and proposals were not *"up to the mark."*

The next morning President Kendrick was informed of a board meeting to be held later in the afternoon. As he walked up the stairs to the meeting, he wished he had worn his blue suit. The meeting was brief and to the point. *"Mike, you just haven't fulfilled the responsibilities of your office. You're a fine administrator; your reorganization of the committee structure and budget was extremely well done, your academic appointments have shown good judgment of character. But you cannot reduce your task to certain areas of responsibility to the exclusion of others. Your primary responsibility as presi-*

dent is to raise university funds. You have apparently relinquished that task to the State and, as a result of your laxity, this institution is in serious financial straits!" There was a long moment of silence. "Therefore, this board has decided to ask for your resignation."

Kendrick had anticipated the blow, but now its implications hit him. "Look, I realize that I have not performed well in this area, but I have some ideas . . ."

"We've examined your past efforts with this," a gray-haired member of the board interrupted, "and considered your present proposals as told to Mr. Forbes. We don't believe our decision is a hasty one."

Kendrick was desperate. Where could he possibly find another position? And after having been fired? And with Ann's mother in the hospital, how could he move his family now?

"Is it possible," he asked, "for me to move into a faculty position? My course work, as you know, was in psychology and counseling, and we could certainly use help in that department."

The room was still, as the board members exchanged glances.

"It will be nearly impossible for me to find another administrative position at this time of the year. My wife's mother has recently had a heart attack and is in the hospital. To move my family now would be a terrible hardship."

"Have your letter of resignation prepared in the morning and we will consider your request," Forbes replied.

It was a sober evening and a sleepless night for Kendrick. "How could I have predicted there would be an oil crisis that would affect the university? What am I supposed to be, some sort of prophet? Ah, but I made a foolish mistake. Even those student demonstrations could have warned me. And John set up those contacts to help me out. Maybe I should give him a call. No, I can't call him—not after he worked so hard to get me the position and then I botched it up like this. I can't face him now. Besides, what would I say? Ask him for another position? Sure! I don't deserve another chance . . . but what am I going to do?"

The following afternoon he signed his resignation as president, and his contract as a part-time professor for one semester. Late in August he found more part-time work as a psychologist at a state hospital outside of town. Between his class and his work at the hospital, he worked many more hours than at his previous position; but it was all necessary to maintain his family. Once he had directed the activities of an entire *university—a microcosm reflecting the richness and diversity of life—but now he waited for late homework assignments, and used a strait jacket to restrain a man's violent aggression.*

Ann's mother lingered on through the cruel winter months. She could barely move. Kendrick felt the same. He had moved from a mansion into a small apartment. Many pieces of furniture had been left in the hall, or sold cheaply. The children felt pressure from their parents' impatience and their arguing behind closed doors at night. The coming of spring seemed to relieve only the heating bills. Kendrick's personal resources were dwindling.

One Friday evening, the doorbell rang unexpectedly. Mike heard Ann greet John Delvin and ask him warmly to come in. For one moment Mike was paralyzed. John had been so instrumental in establishing him as president of Western University that he was ashamed to face him now. But he smiled, and his warm handshake was genuine, for John had been a good friend. Because of his own narrowness of vision, he had lost the position that John had worked so hard for him to receive. Now he sat in his own home across from the man whose confidence and graciousness had allowed him to stretch to the fullest his talents and experience of life. He felt embarrassed about his failure, and yet nothing could adequately express his gratitude for all that John had done for him.

After some general conversation John asked about Mike's plans.

"It's difficult to say," Mike said, as Ann came in with coffee. "With Ann's mother still in the hospital we can't leave, and I've pursued every avenue that has opened up, only to find dead ends. I don't know."

"There may be one possibility you haven't explored." John said.

"What do you mean?" Ann asked.

"Well, it just so happens that the chancellor of State is about to retire. Since I'm the chairman of the board and heading up the committee in search of a replacement . . . well, if you'd be interested, I'd like to see you as chancellor of State University, Mike. What do you think? Would you accept the position?"

Mike was speechless. Ann put her arms around his neck and kissed him on the cheek.

"Well, would you accept the position?" John asked Mike. "It's a larger school than Western and the difficulties are even greater, but I'd like to see you take the challenge. What do you think?"

For a moment fear gripped him as he remembered his firing; but this was replaced by a surge of strength and new-found hope. "I'll take it," he replied firmly, "if you'll work with me on the areas where I need help, and give to me your vision for the university."

John nodded in approval.

"I promise my utmost in service," Mike said. "I promise."

So ends the modern parable. Notice the imagery! The university is the universe. The political science building was missing from Kendrick's window picture of his world; ironically, political science caused his demise. Notice how he cannot draw a circle around his world to keep outside life from affecting him. Note the parallel between Kendrick's downfall and his mother-in-law's health. The wholeness of life is shown by the parallel breakdown in his work and his family life. Leaving the mansion and moving to the apartment characterizes Kendrick's life at that point. Now, John Delvin is a Christ-figure, but the imagery of the story helps us to understand the meaning of restoration. The ending comes as a surprise (even unbelievable), but isn't that like our own surprise in receiving God's grace?

The biblical writers were telling just such stories, but so much time has elapsed since biblical days that their allusions and plays on words escape us.

How could we further develop the story to continue the development of the restoration theme? Perhaps we could have the Kendricks move into a palace. Their marriage would be rejuvenated; their family would find new happiness. The greater responsibilities and benefits of the new job will bring Kendrick joy and satisfaction. Kendrick's mother-in-law could recover, making the point that restoration affects every aspect of our lives in Christ.

Snapshots of a Certain Future

Revelation 21 and 22 paints a vivid picture of a certain future, dispelling the notion that restoration in Christ has meaning only in restricted compartments of our lives. It is not merely our "spiritual" lives which are affected by our redemption; John's vision encompasses a new heaven and a new earth.

> Then I saw a new heaven and a new earth, for the first heaven and the first earth had passed away, and there

was no longer any sea. I saw the Holy City, the new
Jerusalem, coming down out of heaven from God,
prepared as a bride beautifully dressed for her husband. And I heard a loud voice from the throne saying, "Now the dwelling of God is with men, and he
will live with them. They will be his people, and God
Himself will be with them and be their God. He will
wipe every tear from their eyes. There will be no
more death or mourning or crying or pain, for the old
order of things has passed away."

He who was seated on the throne said, "I am making
everything new!" Then he said, "Write this down, for
these words are trustworthy and true."

He said to me: "It is done. I am the Alpha and the
Omega, the Beginning and the End. To him who is
thirsty I will give to drink without cost from the
spring of the water of life. He who overcomes will
inherit all this, and I will be his God and he will be my
son . . . And he carried me away in the Spirit to a
mountain great and high, and showed me the Holy
City, Jerusalem, coming down out of heaven from
God. It shone with the glory of God, and its brilliance
was like that of a very precious jewel, like a jasper,
clear as crystal. It had a great, high wall with twelve
gates, and with twelve angels at the gates. On the
gates were written the names of the twelve tribes of
Israel. There were three gates on the east, three on
the north, three on the south and three on the west.
The wall of the city had twelve foundations, and on
them were the names of the twelve apostles of the
Lamb.

. . . The city was laid out like a square . . . as wide and
high as it is long . . . The wall was made of jasper, and
the city of pure gold, as pure as glass. The foundations of the city walls were decorated with every kind
of precious stone . . . The twelve gates were twelve
pearls, each gate made a single pearl. The street of
the city was of pure gold, like transparent glass.

I did not see a temple in the city, because the Lord
God Almighty and the Lamb are the temple. The city
does not need the sun or the moon to shine on it, for
the glory of God gives it light, and the kings of the
earth will bring their splendor into it. On no day will
its gates ever be shut, for there will be no night there.
The glory and honor of the nations will be brought

into it. Nothing impure will ever enter it, nor will anyone who does what is shameful or deceitful, but only those whose names are written in the Lamb's book of life.

Then the angel showed me the river of the water of life, as clear as crystal, flowing from the throne of God and of the Lamb down the middle of the great street of the city. On each side of the river stood the tree of life, bearing twelve crops of fruit, yielding its fruit every month. And the leaves of the tree are for the healing of the nations. No longer will there be any curse. The throne of God and of the Lamb will be in the city, and his servants will serve him. They will see his face, and his name will be on their foreheads. There will be no more night. They will not need the light of a lamp or the light of the sun, for the Lord God will give them light. And they will reign for ever and ever.[1]

Imagine the excitement! The regal splendor! God's Kingdom is established in all of its completeness, after years of anticipation and struggle. The old created order is changed into the new, and God's people are adorned as the bride of the King's Son. Sorrows are soothed; mourning, crying, and pain are wiped from memory. Thirst is quenched without cost and the longing of God's people is satisfied forever by the immediate presence of God and the Lamb, from whom they draw their meaning and light, their sustenance and healing.

The Alpha, who created all things, is also the Omega, who restores all things. The future is not a return to the garden of Genesis 1. The Revelation imagery of perfection and preciousness says that everything God made in the beginning has been developed and enhanced in the end, despite what had to be overcome.

Revelation 21 and 22 gives us a snapshot of what is in store for the people of God. The Lamb sits on the throne. At other points in the Revelation to John, Christ is seen riding a white stallion or as a warrior with a sword coming out of His mouth. Here, however, John sees the sacrificed Lamb. What better way is there to tie the coming victory of the new heavens and new earth to the death of Christ than by focusing on the Lamb without blemish who was anticipated by the sacrificial system of the Old Covenant? God's people will ultimately overcome because of the death of Christ! It is the Lamb who sits on the throne. Only those whose names are written in the Lamb's book of life will enter into the pictured city. They will no longer experience the curse of sin; instead, they will be His servants and serve Him forever.

As soon as sin entered the world, the restoration of God's people began in anticipation of the death of Christ (Gen. 3:15). The death of Christ guarantees that God's people will indeed experience the full restoration depicted by John at the close of the Revelation. We will not have merely new meaning in our lives, or new clothes, or a new fellowship with God, but we will experience a new order—a renewed world. God's redemption in Christ culminates in the final chapters of Revelation. What He began He will complete; He is the Alpha and the Omega.

Sense the completeness pictured in Revelation 21 and 22! Read it again! Sense the contrast between the paradise pictured in Genesis 1 and 2 and the golden city envisioned in Revelation 21 and 22. The pristine goodness of Genesis has become the "city of God," to use Augustine's phrase. We can be sure that God's faithfulness will finish that which He began.

Hosea: A Vivid Timeless Image

The book of Hosea underlines the grand theme of restoration. The book itself is a life-size dramatization of God's gracious restoration of His people.

God told the prophet Hosea to marry Gomer, not in spite of her immoral ways but because of them. He wanted to demonstrate the depth of divine love and faithfulness through Hosea and his marriage. After bearing three children, Gomer left her husband and family to return to her immorality.[2] And then Hosea went to the slave auction to pay for the return of his unfaithful wife. Understanding this startling image enables us to grasp the meaning of our restoration in Christ. The God who made us for His very own has redeemed us at deep personal cost. He has restored us as full members of His family, refusing to leave us to our own fanciful desires. More than that, He now works within us, through His Spirit, to help us put our whoring ways behind us and to make us a renewed and legitimate bride.

The Breadth of Restoration

The Kendrick story, like the book of Hosea, helps us to understand restoration more clearly. It is important to note that restoration implies a reworking of something, not replacing it with something new. Applied to our lives, this means that God restores us by confirming that which is appropriate within us at salvation. He further develops the appropriate while eradicating the sinful and inappropriate that remains. He does not eliminate every trace of who we are and start building all over again; He molds us beginning with who we are. God remakes our lives just as we might remake antique furniture. He removes the blemishes, tightens up the joints, and brings out the best within us by means of the proper sanding, staining, and finishing by His Spirit.

Restoration does not stop with merely developing our "spiritual lives" or our moral conduct. Revelation 21 and 22 actually signals the elimination of such compartmentalized faith—there is no temple in the golden city! Instead, we see God and the Lamb face to face. Nothing is hidden from His sight. A parallel picture in Zechariah shows that even the cooking pots and horse's bells will be inscribed, "Holy to the Lord" (14:20). In the great and final restoration there will be only that which gives glory to God, and even the common everyday items and events of life will praise Him.

The third stage of creation was described as the developmental stage in which humanity was charged with the responsibility to elicit from the creation all the potential it holds. Men and women were to cultivate the garden, the world in microcosm. After the fall, sin moves down through the three stages of creation. The third stage is still in process; in their work of development, humans attempt to structure reality themselves rather than accept God's structure and working within it. Perverted culture must now be restored, and this happens as redeemed men and women, girls and boys perform their developing tasks. Restored people cannot allow themselves to be shackled by a sinfully structured culture. Restoration is based on redemption in Christ and begins in humanity, but it must be extended throughout all that God has created. Restored structures and societal relations with the creation are used by God to change lives and cultures. The third stage of development must be carried out daily, because now there is double work to do. Restoration begins with our changed hearts and moves through our lives to extend to the very pots in the kitchen and the bells on the horses—". . . the old order of things has passed away" (Rev. 21:4). Perhaps a contemporary illustration would be that both the ovenware and the public transit would give glory to God.

This new order, it must be remembered, is not something substituted for the old; it is the transformation of the old order. The old is not annihilated—it does not cease to exist—but is changed, renewed, reborn, restored, made right, and completed. When the restoration takes place fully, as pictured in Revelation and Zechariah, our present world does not cease to exist and a new one drop from the skies to replace it. Rather, the appropriate things about our present world are confirmed and our efforts to glorify God are completed. The old is made new as everything is restored to its proper place of service to God. This transforming process can be likened to the process by which gold is purified by burning off the dross (I Peter 1:7), or even to the process of trial and temptation that builds perseverance in men and women (James 1:12).

Thus, renewal and restoration have double meanings. First of all, they describe what has happened and will continue to happen in our lives. Our relationship with God has been restored in Christ (II Cor. 5:18-21) and the sanctification process has begun whereby we are conformed to the likeness of Christ and prepared to experience the bliss of the fulfillment as seen in Revelation 21 and 22. Secondly, restoration and renewal describe a privilege and responsibility Christian men and women bear. Just as the process of restoration in us gradually evidences itself in our various activities, so we need to work in all of creation to enhance its renewal. As we do that, faithfully observing the structures God has established, we perform our stated role in the restoration of the world. We know that only God can complete that work when He fulfills the picture of Revelation 21 and 22. Yet the partial restoration we bring will be confirmed then, as well as strengthened and built upon.

This confirming process of restoration can be clarified by an analogy. Suppose that a Nobel Laureate professor at a world-renowned university is likened to God (we will suppose this despite the great differences). He now sub-contracts a select group of students as assistants in a special project for which he has been commissioned. He instructs them all very clearly and sends each to research in an area of his or her own specialty. When they return, he will use their work to produce the final project.

He will begin by sorting through the volumes of efforts done on his behalf. He will quickly eliminate that which was inappropriate or fell too far short of his own high standards. With much of the work, he will spend time to rework it so that it is usable. Some of the material may be done so well that the research needs only minor polishing or sharpening to be strengthened to withstand a challenge. He will then take all of the worthwhile material and weave it together into the perfect product—one that is unmistakably his own.

This analogy demonstrates how the final restoration will take place. Christian men and women everywhere are the select group and the project is the development and restoration of the good creation that God made. He has sent some into each walk of life to work to the best of their ability to contribute to the project. Some have gone into medicine, others into business; some have become teachers, others politicians or clergymen; some were sent out as mothers or fathers, others as carpenters or laborers. If a vocation carries the potential of serving God, then God has called people to be there to demonstrate restoration and to assist in the renewal of that area. One day "the professor," God in Christ, will come to review the work. If a thing was not done in His name it will be banished and replaced with the perfect counterpart. Some things done in His name will need to have radical alterations made, but other things will be strengthened, confirmed, and polished. Christians have been given instructions in the Bible, just as the professor's students received instructions; but Christians also have the advantage that the Holy Spirit goes on before, enlightening and enabling, making it possible for them to do their work appropriately. When God is done reworking, everything will be unmistakably His product. The result will be the fulfillment of the world envisioned in Revelation.

If our own restoration and future are certain because of the life, death, resurrection and ascension of Christ, we ought boldly to assume our responsibility to develop and restore the creation. Neither Kendrick nor Gomer would hesitate to count on their restoration and act accordingly. Kendrick would certainly not stay in his apartment nor keep his lesser jobs when restored to the position of chancellor. Gomer would be able to count on the faithfulness of Hosea forever after he redeemed her from bondage. Christians in our time must be assured of the full restoration that lies ahead so that they may proclaim boldly the restoration that Christ brings now to all of life. We need not fear mistakes, for God will correct them when He confirms what we've done appropriately. There is no valid excuse for not carrying on the developmental task which God has given us. We have the responsibility to restore, with the realization that heaven and earth depend not on our work but on God's grace. We have the responsibility to be obedient; to serve Him who has redeemed us. That duty is a privilege, for He is Lord of all, but servanthood is neither easy nor glamorous—it requires all of our lives.

The closing verse of the book of Daniel charges us appropriately: "As for you, go your way till the end. You will rest, and then at the end of the days you will rise to receive your allotted inheritance" (Dan. 12:13).

Notes

1. Revelation 21:1-7, 10-14, 16a, 16d, 18-19a, 21-27; Revelation 22:1-5.
2. The children of Gomer and Hosea had significant names that enriched the prophetic story. Their names were: Jezreel, remembering the bloodshed there for the people's disobedience; Lo-Ruhamah, meaning "she has not obtained compassion"; and Lo-Ammi, meaning "not my people." These add to the depth of the restoration theme. See Hosea 1-3 for details of the story.

Chapter 4

Restored to Service

S ervanthood is a way of life for Christians, both individually and corporately. Christians are servants or messengers of the Creator and Redeemer of the universe, who served first by giving His life as a ransom for many (Matt. 20:28). The Christian response to the question "Who am I?" is "I am a servant—a servant of the Lord Jesus Christ, to whom I owe my very life." It is no small thing to stand as an ambassador of the God of the universe, as David demonstrated when he confronted the "uncircumcised" Philistine, Goliath. David said to him: "You come against me with sword and spear and javelin, but I come against you in the name of the Lord Almighty, the God of the armies of Israel, whom you have defied. This day the Lord will hand you over to me . . . and the whole world will know that there is a God in Israel . . . for the battle is the Lord's . . ." (I Sam. 17:45-47). As servants for the Lord, Christians battle the powers of darkness; therefore, we must "Put on the full armor of God . . . For our struggle is not against flesh and blood, but against the rulers, against the authorities, against the powers of this dark world and against the spiritual forces of evil in the heavenly realms" (Eph. 6:11, 12). The battlefield is the universe, and the territory to be gained or lost is the whole of creation, visible and invisible. John White points out that a Christian is marked "in the sight of demons and angels as a human who is different.[1] We are soldiers in the army of the Lord, and must live accordingly, allowing the King to govern us in everything.

Paul urges the Christians in Rome ". . . to offer your bodies as living sacrifices, holy and pleasing to God which is your spiritual worship. Do not conform your mind" (Rom.

40

12:1b, 2a). There is an image of death in Paul's allusion to sacrifice—giving one's life in behalf of some loved or important person, national cause, or god. Think of the father who drowns while saving his daughter's life, the secret service agent who leaps in front of bullets to protect a president, or the soldier who dies in battle for his country. To speak of a "living" sacrifice strikes a contrast; and yet the meaning of offering one's life in allegiance remains. Every moment of a Christian's life, whether he or she is engaged in conversation, thinking through a business transaction, shopping at the grocery store, preparing an evening meal, watching television, or reading a novel in bed, should be offered to the Lord. For Christians are to be living, walking, talking, breathing, thinking, feeling sacrifices to the Lord.

I Yam What I Am

Ralph Ellison's great and moving novel, *The Invisible Man*, deals with the matter of self-definition—the identity of the black American, who is a product of two cultures.

In the opening paragraph the protagonist explains his invisibility:

> I am invisible, understand, simply because people refuse to see me. Like the bodiless heads you see sometimes in circus sideshows, it is as though I have been surrounded by mirrors of hard, distorting glass. When they approach me they see only my surroundings, themselves, or figments of their imagination— indeed, everything and anything except me.[2]

The protagonist has no identity of his own; he is defined by what other people think he is. Through a life-journey of anguish and injustice, the hero arrives at a statement of faith in individual autonomy: "This is all very wild and childish, I thought, but to hell with being ashamed of what you're like. No more of that for me. I yam what I am."[3] (The allusion to the book of Exodus, where God identifies Himself to Moses, "I am who I am" (3:14), is obvious.) The black hero finds his identity in his personal freedom and moral responsibility. After buying sweet potatoes, he claims them as his "birthmark" and says, "I yam what I am!"[4] His statement of identity is represented by sweet potatoes, a cultural symbol. His solution to the dilemma of identification is one of complete autonomy, affirming, with Robert Bone, the maxim, "Man is the creator of his own reality."

The early identity of the black American was rooted in his slavery. Frederick Douglass wrote in his nineteenth century work, *Narrative of the Life of Frederick Douglass, An American Slave, Written by Himself:*

> I have found that, to make a contented slave, it is necessary to make a thoughtless one. It is necessary to darken his moral and mental vision, and, as far as possible, to annihilate the power of reason. He must be able to detect no inconsistencies in slavery; he must be made to feel that slavery is right; and he can be brought to that only when he ceases to be a man.[6]

It is a true portrayal of that institution which played so vital a role in American history and influences attitudes and thoughts even today. With this view of slavery so firmly implanted in our North American minds, who would want to be a slave? Yet, this *is* the identity of a Christian. Jesus said to His disciples, "If anyone wants to be first, he must be the very last, and the servant of all" (Mark 9:35). Jesus Himself was the model:

> "Now that I, your Lord and Teacher, have washed your feet, you also should wash one another's feet. I have set you an example that you should do as I have done for you. I tell you the truth, no servant is greater than his master, nor is a messenger greater than the one who sent him. Now that you know these things, you will be blessed if you do them" (John 13:14-17).

Christians are to resist conforming to a society whose highest values are self-reliance and personal peace. Servanthood is at the center of the calling to be a Christian.

You've Got to Serve Somebody

There is at once a point of unity and a measure of diversity in the biblical view of being a servant. First, there is unity in that all people serve somebody or something. Everyone directs his or her life toward some ultimate purpose, some goal, or some accomplishment. Yet the varieties of service are as differentiated as the creation itself. The woman who believes that marriage and family will give meaning to her life will calculate her days on the earth differently than the one who will be satisfied only with fame and fortune. Likewise, the man who believes his life can only be fulfilled by being the president of the company might be willing to sacrifice family and personal relationships as he relocates annually. Another might refuse a raise and promotion in favor of keeping his children in the same school and continuing his family's involvement in their church. Life, you see, is ordered according to what one deems important and/or worthwhile. All activities in life are structured around and submitted to this ultimate concern.

Love—40: Tennis Anyone? One Sunday afternoon during my undergraduate days, my housemates and I were watching a televised tennis tournament. A beautiful woman had just made a spectacular shot to win the final. We all cheered and during the commercial break dreamed out loud about getting a date with her. Later, as I walked to the campus, I imagined what it would be like to date this tennis pro. First, I would have to get up every morning by 7:30 for a tennis lesson, or else I could never stay on the court with her. I'd have to buy a good tennis racket, a Deluxe Super Special 10,000, proper tennis clothes—plenty of white shorts and colored shirts, with the right emblem on the pocket. I'd need other clothes, too; no more corduroys and flannel shirts to the student union dance. But how would I take her out? The poor college student was without a car. Well, if I lessened my class load and got a part-time job, I'd be able to afford a car, a fancy sports car. But car payments can be high and gasoline prices don't get any lower. So maybe I'd drop out of school and work full-time. But dropping out of school and driving a car with only two seats would mean I wouldn't get to spend much time with my friends. But ah, it would all be worth it! I'm in love—and she loves me!

Then I imagined driving one day to her house, sauntering to the door, ringing the bell—and being met by the number-one-ranked male tennis player. I'd cry, "But Sweetheart?" She'd say, "You've been aced!" I'd be "heartbroken," cry in my car all night, and the next morning I'd sleep in and miss my tennis lesson.

What would take place, then, would be nothing less than another total restructuring of my life, a change in every aspect from dress and socializing to car payments and vocation. Priorities would be shifted, and fancy clothes would gather dust in the closet (but I'd probably keep the tennis racket).

When someone sells his heart to someone or something, every action of life becomes a manifestation, proof of purchase, of the sale. The wise man of the Book of Proverbs exhorts his son: "Above all else, guard your heart, for it is the wellspring of life" (Prov. 4:23). Hundreds of biblical references to the "heart" describe it as the principal directing force in an individual's life. "Listen, my son, and be wise, and keep your heart on the right path" (Prov. 23:19). Out of the heart or the principal directing force flow the issues of life, that is, every activity of life. Our thinking, feeling, playing, working, conversing, and even relaxing are directed by the heart. Jesus used the symbol of a tree to demonstrate this:

> "No good tree bears bad fruit, nor does a bad tree bear good fruit. Each tree is recognized by its own fruit. People do not pick figs from thornbushes, or grapes from briers. The good man brings good things out of the evil stored up in his heart. For 'out of the overflow of his heart his mouth speaks' " (Luke 6:43-45).

The activities of life become a manifestation of what lies in the individual's heart. Nothing is excluded from its influence.

Out of the Dragon's Lair. A beautiful illustration of this truth can be found in *The Voyage of "the Dawn Treader,"* an episode of C.S. Lewis' *The Chronicles of Narnia.* Eustace, a disagreeable and unbelieving boy, entered the lair of a dead dragon to find shelter from the rain. Inside he discovered an enormous treasure of "crowns, coins, rings, bracelets, ingots, cups, plates, and gems." Greed welled up inside him, and while pondering how rich and comfortable he could be, he slipped a bracelet onto his arm and fell asleep. Awakened by a terrible pain in his arm, Eustace discovered that "He had turned into a dragon while he was asleep. Sleeping on a dragon's hoard with greedy dragonish thoughts in his heart, he had become a dragon himself." At first he thought that this would be a fine way to get even with his companions.

> But the moment he thought this he realized that he didn't want to. He wanted to be friends. He wanted to get back among humans and talk and laugh and share things. He realized that he was a monster cut off from the whole human race. An appalling loneliness came over him. He began to see the others had not really been friends at all. He began to wonder if he himself had been such a nice person as he had always supposed.

Eustace was turned back into a boy again only when Aslan, the Christ-figure, undressed him and washed him in a clear, bubbling well. Eustace tried to undress himself by scratching away the scaly skin, but only Aslan could undress him. Eustace explained:

> The very first tear he made was so deep that I thought it had gone right into my heart. And when he began pulling the skin off, it hurt worse than anything I've ever felt. The only thing that made me able to bear it was just the pleasure of feeling the stuff peel off.

Lewis made a point of saying that "from that time forth Eustace was a different boy."

One's heart shows itself by those daily activities which are caught in the current flowing from the wellspring of life, the heart. We may see only the outward manifestation of the heart in the way that one lives life, but the Lord looks directly upon the heart: "The Lord does not look at the things man looks at. Man looks at the outward appearance, but the Lord looks at the heart" (I Sam. 16:7b). The Lord knows exactly what it is that drives people to live as they do. He knows that they will use their talents for the sake of it, overcome their faults for it, and see the world and life in light of it. That utmost concern governs the way that they live, determines what they will do and how they will do it, distinguishes right from wrong, and gives them a reason for living, gives meaning to their existence. They become slaves to this highest priority, all other things in life being colored by it.

If you can imagine being taken captive by aliens from another planet and rocketed across the galaxy to some remote world where you can barely communicate, let alone survive, you are beginning to understand how a servant's life is not his or her own. Your master would govern every movement of your life. Paul reminds us that we were purchased by the blood of Christ and are, therefore, "God's possession" (Eph. 1:14): "Do you not know that your body is a temple of the Holy Spirit, who is in you, whom you have received from God? You are not your own; you were bought at a price" (I Cor. 6:19, 20a). "For he who was a slave when he was called by the Lord is the Lord's freedman; similarly, he who was a free man when he was called is Christ's slave. You were bought at a price; do not become slaves of men" (I Cor. 7:22-23). A servant lives his life for the sake of his master. Those who have been ransomed from the kingdom of darkness and are now citizens of the Kingdom of Light must also be workers in that Kingdom.

Actually, to be human is to be a servant, for all people

render their lives in service to some god, which is the essence of religion. John Calvin described humans as being "incurably religious" (*Institutes*, I,3) and Martin Luther said, "What is dear to a man, that is his god" (*Works*, Vol. 21, Pelican, pp. 175-176). The question is not whether someone will be a servant or not but what the direction of that service will be. In the opening chapter of his letter to the Romans, Paul characterizes people according to the direction of their service. There are those who serve the true and living God, and those who have ". . . exchanged the truth of God for a lie, and worshipped and served created things rather than the Creator—who is forever praised" (Rom. 1:25). Those who do not serve the Lord God with all their heart, soul, mind, and strength, serve something that He has created—some part or aspect of the creation. Immediately one thinks of the ancient peoples who worshipped the sun, moon, and stars; but the possibilities for a way of life in service to something within the creation are as unlimited as the imaginations of the heart. For instance, some people believe that accumulating wealth will bring them happiness. Others hope that technology will make enough advances within their lifetime to wipe out cancer and all other human infirmities; they will then be among the first to live forever. Thousands have paid large sums to have their bodies frozen when they die, hoping to be resurrected when the key to immortal life is discovered. Some cling to power and others to romantic love. Some move to the mountains for clean air and others fight against pollution control. Despite the confusion over what is valuable, everyone pledges allegiance to some god and lives his or her life according to its demands.

Warning Against a Divided Allegiance

Inherent in the biblical notion of servanthood is an explicit warning against divided allegiance. Jesus said, "No one can serve two masters. Either he will hate the one and love the other, or he will be devoted to the one and despise the other" (Matt. 6:24a). Just so, the man who tries to please both his wife and his mistress finds that his time and resources, when divided, dwindle to inadequacy. Neither woman can be satisfied when he cannot devote himself fully to either. Tension mounts, and love very quickly turns to hate.

Paul urges Christians ". . . to offer your bodies as living sacrifices . . . Do not conform any longer to the pattern of this world, but be transformed by the renewing of your mind"

(Rom. 12:1, 2). He makes the issue of divided service clear to the Galatians:

> Formerly, when you did not know God, you were slaves to those who by nature are not gods. But now that you know God—or rather are known by God— how is it that you are turning back to those weak and miserable principles? Do you wish to be enslaved by them all over again? (Gal. 4:8, 9).

Nothing a man or woman does or thinks is hidden from God's sight (Ps. 139). All of the diversity and complexity of life is a product of His imaginative creating. Though we deserve death, we have life, abundant and eternal, because we were purchased at the price of Christ's blood. We live because He died, and in the knowledge of this Paul said: "I have been crucified with Christ and I no longer live, but Christ lives in me. The life I live in the body, I live by faith in the Son of God, who loved me and gave himself for me" (Gal. 2:20). A life that is true to the way things really are in the universe is a life that is lived as a total sacrifice, in complete submission to the Maker of heaven and earth.

Paul cautions us: "You were bought at a price; do not become slaves of men" (I Cor. 7:23). We must resist the temptation to divide the offering of our lives between two gods. No human creature can pledge allegiance to the God of the universe and rightfully bow down in adoration before another creature or thing:

> "You shall have no other gods before me. You shall not make for yourself an idol in the form of anything in heaven above or on the earth beneath or in the waters below. You shall not bow down to them or worship them; for I, the Lord your God, am a jealous God . . ." (Ex. 20:3-5a).

The covenantal imagery of Scripture portrays God as a lover, wooing and caressing His people, but jealously angry when they flirt and chase after other gods. As Christians we must always be asking whose territory we are expanding. The acts we perform and the decisions we make constantly display the committed service of our hearts. We are either being ". . . conformed to the likeness of His Son . . ." (Rom. 8:29) by God's Spirit, or as the psalmist tells us, if we serve an idol: "Those who make them will be like them, and so will all who trust in them" (Ps. 115:8). We have to be on our guard or, like Eustace, we might start breathing fire.

There is a story about a newly committed Christian who climbed a high mountain. He stood on the edge of a cliff to admire God's handiwork in the breathtaking view below. Suddenly the edge of the cliff collapsed. He began to fall, but managed to grab a branch growing out of the cliffside. He looked down and saw rocks and dirt land miles below in a cloud of dust. His arm was tiring, and he shouted in desperation, "Help! Help! Is anybody up there?! Is anybody up there?! God! Are You up there?"

God's booming voice answered, "I'm here. Let go of the branch."

The man yelled, "God! God! Is that You up there?"

God answered, "I'm here. Let go of the branch and I'll lift you up."

Clutching the branch, the man looked up and then down and hollered, "Is anybody else up there?"

There is security in hanging on to what we can see and touch. We always feel safer in familiar surroundings. Rural children laugh at the "city kids" when they are at camp together. In the dead of night a twig snaps and they huddle together crying, "Tigers! Bears!" But drop those "country kids" off on a street corner in downtown Pittsburgh at two in the morning and the sound of a tin can on the street means "Mugger! Rapist!"

To achieve tangible security, the people of Israel continually sought after the idols, the false gods of the surrounding nations. They sought idols which Jeremiah said were "Like a scarecrow in a melon patch . . ."—that is, deaf, dumb, and blind; and which Isaiah referred to as ". . . gods that cannot save" (Jer. 10:5 and Is. 45:20). Through the prophet Isaiah, God spoke to His people concerning this:

> "When you cry out for help,
>   let your collection of idols save you!
> The wind will carry all of them off,
>   a mere breath will blow them away,
> But the man who makes me his refuge
>   will inherit the land
>   and possess my holy mountain" (Is. 57:13).

I wonder if our cliff-hanger ever read that passage in Isaiah? Still, it is difficult to let go of what seems so safe and secure. It is hard to follow God's leading into the wilderness as Abraham did (Gen. 12). However, the promise is that those who trust the Lord will inherit the land and possess His holy mountain. For those people, life will be as it was meant to be

—healthy, enriched, and fulfilled. For those who compromise their trust and who address another god even on a certain issue, Isaiah points out that ". . . the things they treasure are worthless" (Is. 44:9b).

The task of living obediently looks awesome when we consider all of the kinds of possibilities God has created for us to unfold and develop. They include, for example, understanding the geology of the planet earth, finding creative ways of enriching family life, teaching methods of nurturing children, and exploring the imaginative realm of fiction. In our daily activities as servants and messengers of the Lord, we might ask if magazine ads and television commercials are teaching us that goods and products are in service to God and our neighbor, or are we being taught that our worldly possessions are status symbols? When we cast our vote on election day, do we vote for a political leader who will keep his campaign promises and will seek to execute justice, or for one who has paid a media-man to sell him to the public? Do the movies we watch for entertainment reveal allusively the truth about the way things are, or are they propaganda for a salvation rooted in man? Do we know how to tell the difference? We have to learn to be able to discern the threads which weave the tapestry of life. To appeal to any authority for understanding other than to the Lord is to appeal to an idol.

The psalmist's reminder that "The earth is the Lord's, and everything in it, the world, and all who live in it" (Ps. 24:1) emphasizes the stewardly responsibilities of the Christian servant to care for, direct, and develop all that God has made. An overwhelming task? A heavy burden? Remember the words of Jesus:

> "Take my yoke upon you and learn from me, for I am gentle and humble in heart, and you will find rest for your souls. For my yoke is easy and my burden is light" (Matt. 1:29, 30).

As a gentle teacher, Jesus will help us understand the world and life He has given to us. Our aim is perfect obedience in all that we do. We seek to do the will and the bidding of God. Jesus made the cost of discipleship clear:

> ". . . If anyone would come after me, he must deny himself and take up his cross daily and follow me. For whoever wants to save his life will lose it, but whoever loses his life for me will save it. What good

is it for a man to gain the whole world, and yet lose
or forfeit his very self?" (Luke 9:23-25).

What is involved is our very selves; we are to be living
sacrifices. That is our identity—servants of the Lord Jesus
Christ, to whom we owe our very existence.

The temptation, however, is to reduce the response of our
whole life, our living offering, to certain activities of life,
usually those in the realms of personal morality and conduct.
Then we view other activities as outside of the realm of Christian consideration, or relegate them to strictly defined areas
of personal morality. For instance, we consider people in "the
ministry" to be full-time Kingdom workers, while people in
other occupations are "part-time" servants. Our Christian
faith is related to our work only when we have an opportunity
to invite our co-worker to a Bible study or share our faith. The
Bible is seen as irrelevant to issues concerning the nature of
work or to specific business practices.

Ironically, if we ignore the world around us we might find
ourselves slaves to it. If we relinquish our task (Gen. 1:28) and
do not use the earth and its fullness in the name of the Lord,
others will use it in the name of some other god. Because the
earth is our dwelling place, there is no way to escape the work
of those who serve idols; nor should we want to escape. God
gave us this dwelling place and called it good. If we let our
God-given home be shaped, designed, and patterned after
idols, we must face the consequences. Here are two examples.

Think of a teenage girl who works on weekends to be able
to buy the latest fashions. Exercising hard to develop her
coordination and keep her lean body in shape, she becomes a
member of the cheerleading squad and is voted homecoming
queen in her senior year. She brings home only A's and B's
and gets a part in the school musical. Think of how hurt and
surprised her Christian parents are when she staggers in
drunk on Saturday night, and how shocked they are when she
confesses that the birth-control pills are hers and that sex is a
regular part of her dating pattern—all for the sake of
popularity. Remember God's Word in the Psalms:

> . . . but they mingled with the nations
>   and adopted their customs.
> They worshipped their idols
>   which became a snare to them.
> They sacrificed their sons
>   and their daughters to demons.

> They shed innocent blood,
>> the blood of their sons and daughters,
> whom they sacrificed to the idols of Canaan,
>> and the land was desecrated by their blood.
> They defiled themselves by what they did;
>> by their deeds they prostituted themselves
>> (Ps. 106:35-39).

How many believing parents abandon the full responsibility of nurturing their children—of inspiring them, by precept and example, to serve the Lord? How many of these same parents allow cigarette ads, the security of the latest fashions, the perspectives of film directors, and far-reaching decisions of politicians to play key roles in influencing their children's behavior and life styles? Jesus said, "No one can serve two masters. Either he will hate the one and love the other, or he will be devoted to the one and despise the other."

Think of the Christian gentleman who stands up in front of a church filled with people from his local community, and testifies for half an hour about the way "the Lord" broke him of his cigarette habit. With the money he saved he bought a new set of golf clubs. He wears brand-name three-piece suits to work, has struggled to climb the ladder of his company, and is well respected in the community. He spends time with his family, taking them on expensive vacations, and gives money to foreign missions. In the back row of the church this morning sits a group of students who rent apartments from this Christian gentleman. They have come to hear him speak. These students pay high rent for their apartments which are located on the edge of campus. The roofs leak and the water runs down the paint-peeling walls. The wind blows through in the winter. There is always a long wait for repairs, and in the summer an assortment of insects vacation there. Student housing is difficult to find, and they have to pay for it. This Christian gentleman stopped smoking—all for the sake of maximizing his profit.

How many Christian businessmen bow down before the law of the maximization of profit? Do our twentieth-century Christian business endeavors demonstrate the wisdom and glory of God as did the sabbatical system or the year of Jubilee? Is there room in our modern world for economic reconciliation which reflects the mercy we know as sinners reconciled to the Father by the Son's death? Who are we? We are servants of the Lord Jesus Christ, to whom we owe our very lives. Jesus said, "No one can serve two masters. Either he will hate the one and love the other, or he will be devoted to the one and despise the other."

Try to Learn What Is Pleasing to the Lord

Wisdom and understanding are two marks of a servant of the Lord—"The fear of the Lord is the beginning of wisdom, and knowledge of the Holy One is understanding" (Prov. 9:10). A servant of the Lord is to see and discern like Solomon (see I Kings 3:16-28). Paul explains to the Colossians the significance of these characteristics:

> . . . we have not stopped praying for you and asking God to fill you with the knowledge of his will through all spiritual wisdom and understanding. And we pray this in order that you may live a life worthy of the Lord and may please him in every way: bearing fruit in every good work, growing in the knowledge of God, being strengthened with all power according to his glorious might so that you may have great endurance and patience, and joyfully giving thanks to the Father, who has qualified you to share in the inheritance of the saints in the kingdom of light (Col. 1:9b-12).

Christians need to be praying constantly for wisdom and understanding, for although the battle in our daily lives involves flesh-and-blood decisions and actions, the backdrop is a struggle ". . . against the powers of this dark world and against the spiritual forces of evil in the heavenly realms" (Eph. 6:12b). We must cultivate and use the wisdom and understanding that God has given us—in even the simplest decisions, like what kind of sugar to buy—if we want the Lord to say to us, as the master in the parable said, "Well done, good and faithful servant! You have been faithful with a few things; I will put you in charge of many things. Come and share your master's happiness!" (Matt. 25:21).

Like a runner in a relay race, poised to run when the baton touches his palm, so must we be eager servants, anxious to serve our Lord; waiting quietly at the door of Wisdom, listening for her voice:

> "Listen to my instruction and be wise;
>   do not ignore it.
> Blessed is the man who listens to me,
>   watching daily at my doors,

　　　waiting at my doorway.
　For whoever finds me finds life
　　and receives favor from the Lord.
　But whoever fails to find me harms himself;
　　all who hate me love death" (Prov. 8:33-36).

We need God-given wisdom to understand the meaning of being reconciled to God through Christ; we must be restored to our proper place in His creation as stewards in the name of Christ. Paul continues in his explanation to the Colossians:

> Once you were alienated from God and were enemies in your minds because of your evil behavior. But now he has reconciled you by Christ's physical body through death to present you holy in his sight, without blemish and free from accusation—if you continue in your faith, established and firm, not moved from the hope held out in the gospel. This is the gospel that you heard and that has been proclaimed to every creature under heaven, and of which I, Paul, have become a servant (Col. 1:21-23).

Christians are servants to the Lord, "holy in his sight, without blemish and free from accusation"—in short, forgiven. In rescuing us from the dominion of darkness, God has freed us from our blindness and bondage to sin. God has freed us to see and serve Him with all joy and gladness. This is the gospel of which Paul has become a servant. This is the truth about the way things really are in the universe. Life is true life only when it is lived as an offering to the Maker of heaven and earth. So we should sing songs and encourage one another ". . . in order that you may live a life worthy of the Lord and may please him in every way . . ." (Col. 1:10).

Notes

1. John White, *The Fight* (Downers Grove, IL: InterVarsity Press, 1976), p. 12.
2. Ralph Ellison, *The Invisible Man* (1947; rpt. New York: Random House Vintage, 1972), p. 3.
3. Ellison, p. 259.
4. Ellison, p. 260.
5. Robert Bone, "Ralph Ellison and the Uses of the Imagination," in *Ralph Ellison: A Collection of Essays*, ed. John Hersey (New Jersey: Prentice-Hall, Inc., 1974), p. 104.

6. Frederick Douglass, *Narrative of the Life of Frederick Douglass, An American Slave, Written by Himself*, ed. Benjamin Quarles (Cambridge, MA: Belknap Press, 1960), p. 133.

7. Gordon J. Spykman, *Christian Faith in Focus* (Grand Rapids, MI: Baker Book House, 1967), p. 11.

Chapter 5

Daily Obedience in the Activities of Life—I

A s they sat on the Mount of Olives, the disciples asked Jesus "What will be the sign of your coming at the end of the age?" (Matt. 24:3). After a description of what would happen, Jesus charged them: "Therefore keep watch, because you do not know on what day your Lord will come" (Matt. 24:42). The series of parables that follow instruct them as to the nature of their task until Jesus returns. Each contrasts the faithful and wise servant with the wicked and slothful one. To the servant who had administered his gifts properly the master said: "Well done, good and faithful servant! You have been faithful with a few things; I will put you in charge of many things. Come and share your master's happiness!" (Matt. 25:21). How beautiful those words must sound. The reward for his faithful service is wider responsibility over the master's property. But the worthless servant hears only the stern voice of justice; he is cast into the outer darkness where his servanthood is taken away from him. How are we to understand this in light of our twentieth century experience?

In the first chapter of his letter to the Colossians, the apostle Paul describes the state of affairs for believers after the death, resurrection, and ascension of Christ. God "has rescued us from the dominion of darkness and brought us into the kingdom of the Son he loves, in whom we have redemption, the forgiveness of sins. Once you were alienated from God and were enemies in your minds because of your evil behavior. But now he has reconciled you by Christ's physical body through death to present you holy in his sight, without blemish and free from accusation." Christ is "the image of the

invisible God, the firstborn over all creation." All things were
created by Him and for Him and "God was pleased to have all
his fullness dwell in him, and through him to reconcile to
himself all things, whether things on earth or in heaven, by
making peace through his blood, shed on the cross." The
Christ described in this passage sounds like the "craftsman"
in the delightful account of creation which Proverbs 8:22-31
gives us. Christ is the focus of God's acts of creation and
redemption. As servants who desire Christ's favor, we must
be responsible for all that He entrusts to us.

The prophet Isaiah tells us what the Lord says:

> ". . . he who created the heavens,
>   he is God;
> he who fashioned and made the earth,
>   he founded it;
> he did not create it to be empty,
>   but formed it to be inhabited—
> he says:
>   'I am the Lord, and there is no other . . .' "
>   (Is. 45:18).

What are God-fearing inhabitants of the earth supposed to do
with that knowledge? What should be the focus and direction
of our activity when we have been transferred from the reign
of darkness into the reign of light—freed from a passionate
slavery to sin? Dr. Calvin Seerveld explains:

> God is the focus of a man or woman's life who is freed
> from the divisive finagling of sin. You do things not
> to improve yourself, but to make *God* happy. You
> sweat not to save the "souls" of people, but to bring
> the lives of individual men and women, families, in-
> stitutional leaders, society, under the convicting rule
> of the Word of *God*. You work in this world not to
> make it a better place to live in, but to have it demon-
> strate the wisdom and glory of *God*. From God and
> through God and to God let all things be done for
> ever and ever, amen—that's it! Followers of Christ
> live *for God's sake*.[1]

Christ's substitutionary atonement for sin sets the believer
free to love the Lord with all his or her heart, soul, mind, and
strength, because "God so loved the world that he gave his one
and only Son . . ." (John 3:16).

The life of the believer ought to be one of gratitude. Men

and women who profess the name of Christ have the God-ordained task to care for and cultivate in loving service to the Lord, their lives, their neighbors' lives, and the earth—all of which belong to the Lord. Seerveld asks:

> How can a believer in the Lord respond in any other way than fully, unconditionally, totally, bodily, world-widely to accept cultivation of the earth and all human activities as a ministry that is our logical service? Remembering the mercies of God . . . How can any believer not offer *all* he or she has, sexual drives, artistic talents, professional interests, even sorrows, offer all he or she is, along with all of creation, as a living, passionately smoking sacrifice up to the Lord.[2]

God created and reconciled to Himself all things through Christ. All of our daily activities on the earth ought to be imbued with the light of redemption. Not only our personal lives, but the marketplace, our businesses, our families, our educational institutions, television programing, films, music, our leisure time, furniture, the clothes we wear, and even our landscaping should demonstrate the wisdom and glory of God. For, as the psalmist reminds us, ". . . all things serve you (God)" (Ps. 119:91b).

Recently, I addressed a group of high school students on the very popular topic of self-image. I explained to them that one's identity lies in whom he or she serves while carrying out the activities of life. Knowingly or unknowingly, people are "living sacrifices" to the god they choose to worship with their lives. Christians, I explained, have been restored to their proper place in God's created world; that's why they should live out of sheer gratitude to the true God. With every activity we should ask, "Whom am I serving? Whose territory am I expanding?" We are to be restored, living sacrifices to the Lord Jesus Christ. Following one of my presentations, a young lady approached me rather shyly and said, "But the problem with living sacrifices is that they keep getting off the altar." I laughed, of course, but I also realized that she was looking for some answers to her questions about being a servant of Christ. I had asked those same kinds of questions early in my Christian life. I knew that I was forgiven by God and restored to my proper place in His world, but it took time for me to understand the fullness of being a living offering.

I remember that when I first became a Christian in college it took "only" three months to "perfect my faith." I merely changed my dating patterns, removed all foul words from my vocabulary, stopped getting drunk, had a devotional time every day, had regular fellowship, made it to church every Sunday, and began doing personal evangelism. But I began to notice that my sociology professor did not attribute the problems of society to the corruption of sin; nor did the life, death, and resurrection of Jesus Christ seem to have much relevance to my history class. The breakdown of the family meant that as an institution it should be replaced; education was for the betterment of a "man-made" society; biology glorified the classification of things, ignoring the significance and diversity of God's creatures. No textbook taught that all things are God's servants. I began to discover that the implications for my faith were far-reaching and I began to glimpse the necessity of being a servant of Christ in His good, but fallen, world. I began to sense the breadth of such a commitment. But how could I express it, live it out? Harry Blamires describes the dilemma:

> There is no longer a Christian mind . . . as a *thinking* being, the modern Christian has succumbed to secularization. He accepts religion—its morality, its worship, its spiritual culture, but he rejects the religious view of life, the view which sets all earthly issues within the context of the eternal, the view which relates all human problems—social, political, cultural—to the doctrinal foundations of the Christian Faith, the view which sees all things here below in terms of God's supremacy and earth's transitoriness, in terms of Heaven and Hell.[3]

Aside from matters of personal morality and conduct, Christians have abandoned God's world to be cared for and developed by those who do not serve Him, but who serve created things instead. *They* decorate the earth which the meek will someday inherit (Matt. 5); *they* prescribe the cures for life that has been infected with sin, and *they* shape the direction that civilization will take. Christians have no choice but to live in the world unbelievers are re-creating. As a result, our lives become schizophrenic. We identify evil with created things such as movies, television, alcoholic beverages, cigarettes, and sexuality, rather than understand sin as a power which grips the hearts of men and women and the social structures they create. If we avoid certain "sinful" things, then, we can feel righteous. But then whose territory are we expanding?

The psalmist knowingly asks: "How can a young man

keep his way pure? By living according to your word" (Ps. 119:9). Living according to the Word of God is an enormous task encompassing all that we do. Anything we think or do that is not in accordance with His Word is sin—a violation of our covenantal vow—betraying us as unfaithful servants. Sinful acts destroy life, while acts of obedience make life what it ought to be.

Paul exhorts the Corinthians: "So whether you eat or drink or whatever you do, do it all for the glory of God" (I Cor. 10:31). As Calvin Seerveld points out, Christians "cannot help but be busy culturally: since this is our Father's world, our cultivation of it must show we love Him and recognize that all here belongs to Him."[4] We are to be faithful partners in covenant with God, striving to live lives which reveal the characteristics of a genuine covenant partner. For instance, our judgments—whether they render a courtroom verdict of guilty or not guilty, or merely a decision as to which child can play with the toy next—should illustrate righteousness. *The New Bible Dictionary* defines righteousness as "conformity to law, especially to the law, mind, and will of God, which is the norm for righteousness."[5] H.M. Kuitert points out that the Israelites spoke of things as being righteous:

> A "righteous" way is a way that brings one to where he wants to go and a "righteous" scale is one that works accurately. In both instances the word "righteous" points to a thing that functions properly, meets its purpose; a thing is justified, therefore, if it does what one may expect it to do.[6]

A righteous Christian life is, then, a life offered in service to God to cultivate the world that belongs to Him: "But seek his kingdom, and these things will be given to you as well" (Luke 12:31). As God's covenant partners, Christians are to model the attributes of God, demonstrating His wisdom and glory in a world filled with strangers to His covenant. In our business dealings and international policy we should perform acts of justice, securing the rights of our neighbor and hurrying to help the oppressed. "But let justice roll on like a river, righteousness like a never-failing stream!" the prophet Amos cried (5:24). Our relationships with friends, parents, spouse, co-workers, and those with whom we do business, should be characterized by truth—reliability, dependability, trustworthiness, and consistency in word and deed. In all that we do we are to be signposts, pointing strangers in the way of the

Creator, the glorious God of the covenant "in whom we have redemption, the forgiveness of sins."

What does it mean to be a genuine Christian "signpost"? Should we mount soapboxes on street corners shouting the message of salvation to passersby? . . . pray before a meal at a public restaurant? . . . leave booklets explaining the steps to God as a tip for the waitress' service? . . . invite someone to a Bible study? . . . or play a "Christian" album for them? There is much more to being authentic about the Christian faith than merely proclaiming the Gospel verbally. Certainly the manner and style of our proclaiming is also a reflection of the God we represent. All of our daily activities are woven together like a tapestry and presented as one whole offering to the Lord. In every activity of life we are to act as obedient partners of the Lord, giving those who live in darkness a taste of the holy God of truth, righteousness, and justice. Our lives as Christians must be authentic through and through, or else we are liars.

> The man who says, "I know him," but does not do what he commands is a liar, and the truth is not in him. But if anyone obeys his word, God's love is truly made complete in him. This is how we know we are in him. Whoever claims to live in him must walk as Jesus did (I John 2:4-6).

Here John explains that obedience demonstrates that we know God and that His love is in us.

In *The Timeless Moment*, D. Bruce Lockerbie metaphorically illustrates the genuineness of being a Christian by developing an analogy involving art:

> A conversation with a potter comes to mind. He had asked: If it were possible to make a "Christian pitcher," what would it look like? How would it differ from any other vessel used to pour beverages? We agreed from the outset that no such container existed, but for the sake of discussion we could make these hypothetical suggestions. First, such a piece of pottery holds whatever liquid it contains without leaking. This pitcher stands firmly on its base without tipping over. It may be of almost any shape imaginable, so long as it fulfills its intended purpose to serve as a pitcher. It is what it is, without apology or explanation. Therefore, it needs no emblems to mark it as "Christian." In fact, anything external to its

grace as an object and its function as a utensil is mere advertising or propaganda, not art. We also agreed that it is unthinkable to consider praising the Lord, no matter how boldly the message is inscribed, with a flawed or faulty pitcher.[7]

Christians are not merely to label themselves "Christian" but to be genuine about their lives in faith. We are to be righteous, true to our calling and purpose on the earth, modeling life as it was meant to be lived from the beginning. Paul's concluding exhortation to the Philippians outlines the distinctive qualities of the Christian's activities:

> Finally, brothers, whatever is true, whatever is noble, whatever is right, whatever is pure, whatever is lovely, whatever is admirable—if anything is excellent or praiseworthy—think about such things. Whatever you have learned or received or heard from me, or seen in me—put it into practice. And the God of peace will be with you (Phil. 4:8, 9).

The Daily Worker

Christianity is more than just a fire insurance policy which prevents one from burning in the end; Jesus is the Lord of life on this earth. Douglas Hyde depicts the import of what it means to be fully committed to a vision of life in his book *Dedication and Leadership.* Hyde was the news editor of the London *Daily Worker* and had been a member of the Communist Party for twenty years when he renounced Communism and converted to the Christian faith. Here he describes a day in the life of a dedicated man:

> Often, ex-Communists meeting together can talk of the "old days when we were in the Party" rather like old soldiers discussing nostalgically the campaigns they shared in the past. We had been doing this. We had talked of old comrades who now saw themselves as our enemies, of the campaigns in which we were engaged together.
>
> Then, very wistfully, he said: "Do you remember what life was really like in the Party? You got up in the morning and as you shaved you were thinking of the jobs you would do for Communism that day. You went down to breakfast and read the *Daily Worker* to get the Party line—to get the shot and shell for a

fight in which you were already involved. You read every item in the paper wondering how you might be able to use it for the cause.

"I had never been interested in sport but I read the sports pages in order to be able to discuss sport with others and to be able to say to them, 'Have you read this in the *Daily Worker*?' I would follow this through by giving them the paper in the hope that they might turn from the sports pages and read the political ones too.

"On the bus or train, on my way to work, I read the *Daily Worker* as ostentatiously as I could, holding it up so that others might read the headlines and perhaps be influenced by them. I took two copies of the paper with me; the second one I left on the seat in the hope that someone would pick it up and read it.

"When I got to work, I kept the *Daily Worker* circulating. One worker after another would take it outside, read it for a few minutes and bring it back to me again. At lunchtime, in the canteen or the restaurant, I would try to start conversations with those with whom I was eating. I made a practice of sitting with different groups in order to spread my influence as widely as I could. I did not thrust Communism down their throats but steered our conversations in such a way that they could be brought round to politics or, if possible, to the campaigns which the Party was conducting at the time.

"Before I left my place of work at night, there was a quick meeting of the factory group or cell. There we discussed in a few minutes the successes and failures of the day. And we discussed, too, what we hoped to be able to do on the following day.

"I dashed home, had a quick meal and then went out, maybe to attend classes, maybe to be a tutor, maybe to join some Communist campaign, going from door to door canvassing or standing at the side of the road selling Communist papers—doing something for Communism. And I went home at night and dreamed of the jobs I was going to do for Communism the next day."

Rather sadly he added: "You know, life had some meaning and some purpose in those days. Life was good in the Communist Party."

He was right. Of course it was. It is quite wrong

to suppose that it is only the saints who are not sad. Sinners can get quite a lot of fun out of life too. And those who are dedicated get immensely more out of life than those who are not. The day he described had been my life and that of most of my old comrades. It was a day in the life of a dedicated man, a normal day in the life of a hard-core Communist Party member. It is not surprising that he looked back at that life from the wasteland of his present purposeless existence with a considerable degree of nostalgia (pp. 22-24).

In the opening chapter Hyde writes: "We shall be looking at the Communists, not in order to attack, not to prove them wrong, but rather to see what they have to teach us" (p. 9). Though he has completely rejected the Communist Party's ideology and action, he has found them to be right on some points.

> For example, when they said that there is a great battle going on all over the world which in the final analysis is a struggle for men's hearts, minds, and souls. We can accept this even if we do not take the view that all the "goodies" are on one side and the "baddies" are on the other. There is plenty of evidence that the thought of millions today is in a state of flux, people everywhere are breaking away from age-old allegiances, beliefs, and ways of life, and it is much too early yet to say where the process will finish (p. 10).

When we consider the goal of the Communists—to make the world a Communist world—and that they have achieved one-third of their objective in the past half-century, we have to recognize and examine the dedication and action of their followers.

A song lyric written by John Lennon and Paul McCartney describes a day in the life of another man. Appearing on the album *Sergeant Pepper's Lonely Hearts Club Band*, the song was composed near the end of the turbulent sixties and reflects the frustration of youth who search for meaningful lives. The song and album have become landmarks in rock culture and remain an important memory in popular culture, even to present youth. The lyric tosses off random, unrelated events to illustrate the fragmented absurdity of daily life.

"A Day in the Life"
I read the news today oh boy
about a lucky man who made the grade
and though the news was rather sad
well I just had to laugh
I saw the photograph.
He blew his mind out in a car
he didn't notice that the lights had changed
a crowd of people stood and stared
they'd seen his face before
nobody was really sure
if he was from the House of Lords.
I saw a film today oh boy
the English Army had just won the war
a crowd of people turned away
but I just had to look
having read the book.
I'd love to turn you on.
Woke up, got out of bed,
dragged a comb across my head
found my way downstairs and drank a cup,
and looking up I noticed I was late.
Found my coat and grabbed my hat
made the bus in seconds flat
found my way upstairs and had a smoke,
and somebody spoke and I went into a dream.
I heard the news today oh boy
four thousand holes in Blackburn, Lancashire
and though the holes were rather small
they had to count them all
now they know how many holes it takes
to fill the Albert Hall.
I'd love to turn you on.

The hopelessness comes from the conviction that life is what we see—the superficial, the absurd, the material. Life has no purpose. How this picture differs from the purposeful day in Hyde's description! The apostle Paul tells us of *purpose* in his letter to the Colossians: God created all things, upholds all things, and is reconciling all things to Himself through Christ. God is purposefully leading all things to their ordained conclusion, which extends beyond the grave. Therefore, all activity on the earth is meaningful; the consequences of every thought and deed are seen in the light of the eternal and the work of Christ. Life on earth matters!

Tie Them as Symbols on Your Hands

> See, I have taught you decrees and laws as the
> Lord my God commanded me, so that you may follow
> them in the land you are entering to take possession
> of it. Observe them carefully, for this will show your
> wisdom and understanding to the nations, who will
> hear about all these decrees and say, "Surely this
> great nation is a wise and understanding people."
> What other nation is so great as to have their gods
> near them the way the Lord our God is near us when-
> ever we pray to him? And what other nation is so
> great as to have such righteous decrees and laws as
> this body of laws I am setting before you today?
>
> Only be careful, and watch yourselves closely so
> that you do not forget the things your eyes have seen
> or let them slip from your heart as long as you live.
> Teach them to your children and to their children
> after them (Deut. 4:5-9).

Here, in the book of Deuteronomy, Moses has summa-
rized and spelled out Israel's history, relating the events to
the lessons God intended for His people to learn. In a moving
farewell speech, Moses calls Israel to trust the Lord whole-
heartedly and to make His law the standard for life. If they
observe the law, blessings will follow and all the nations will
see that Israel is distinctive among them and that her God is
the Lord. This is a beautiful moment in God's work of redemption. Hendrik Hart explains its historical significance:

> It is the record of God reschooling, reeducating man-
> kind in the art of living, of being man, of being God's
> key servant in His covenant creation.
>
> Since his fall in Adam, man has already begun to
> die and no longer knows God, no longer understands
> His Word, no longer lives in obedience. And now the
> merciful and faithful Lord of the covenant chooses
> Israel to again make known His ordinances of life.
> The Word that had been so plain in the beginning,
> that was written all over creation, is now going to be
> taught by a loving Father to His blind child. Letter
> for letter the meaning of the Word that gives life is
> spelled out to them in what is called the Law: the
> statutes, ordinances and commandments of the cove-
> nant. Every phase of life is covered; trade and com-

merce, agriculture, rites and rituals, justice between people, family and marriage, education, personal hygiene, etc. Even land and animals are included. (Cf. Exodus through Deuteronomy.) Indeed, the New Humanity begins to take shape in Israel under the watchful eye of God Himself.[8]

During Israel's journey in the wilderness, God taught His people the Law and commanded them to teach their children and their children's children.

> Fix these words of mine in your hearts and minds; tie them as symbols on your hands and bind them on your foreheads. Teach them to your children, talking about them when you sit at home and when you walk along the road, when you lie down and when you get up. Write them on the door frames of your houses and on your gates, so that your days and the days of your children may be many in the land that the Lord swore to give your forefathers, as many as the days that the heavens are above the earth (Deut. 11:18-21).

The results of such education are clear in this passage—life, and life abundant. However, disobedience to the Lord, following and serving other gods, incites the anger of a jealous God, ". . . and his anger will burn against you, and he will destroy you from the face of the land" (Deut. 6:15b). Do we take seriously the Word of the Lord, the Law for life? The consequences are serious. What is the meaning of the Law for Christians in the twentieth century?

Looking at our contemporary setting through the lens of Deuteronomy, we will begin with a detailed discussion of education. Education touches all of our lives when we are students, and then again when we are professionals, parents, or taxpayers. During a time of crisis in public education, when battles rage over "prayer" or "humanism" in the classroom, when alternative schooling is on the rise, accompanied by concerns about the "quality" of education and about segregation, we do well to try to understand the pressing questions *as Christians*. After looking at education, we will move on to briefer discussions of the meaning of the law for vocation, business and economics, leisure and lifestyle.

Teach Them to Your Children

There is not a moment in our daily activity when we are not to be leading our children. Are we leading them in the way of the Lord?

The role of education in society has developed over the ages. A survey of its development would span centuries, covering education as "mere training in the home and in the field, shop, and army" to "a formal training of pupils by professional educators on elementary, secondary, and advanced levels."[9] Today, formal education is in school classrooms.

We are to serve the Lord in all that we do and have dominion over His creation, responsibly seeing to it that "all things are His servants." The education or nurturing of our children is no exception. Every dimension of it is decisively religious, betraying a commitment to a law—someone's word for what is the right way of life. Education is never neutral or impartial. It is an area of service, and service is always purposefully or unpurposefully directed either to God or some false idol.

What is the purposeful direction of American education? The National Education Association (N.E.A.), the largest and oldest association of educators in our country, said that education is important because it "nourishes the underlying values upon which State and Society depend for their existence."[10] These values are those of the American democratic way of life, equality, and freedom—"life, liberty, and the pursuit of happiness." Are they Christian values?

> In North America the state *believes* in the democratic way of life. Note well, not the democratic way of government but of life. A religious vision for life; a vision of how people should live. The guiding principles of this way of life is that a great society, a new humanity, must be forged on the basis of those beliefs that all men of good will—all reasonable men —hold in common. To achieve this commonness every citizen is urged, even forced, to confine his personal religious beliefs to his private world. The democratic way of life is living as *a new community*, a community where atheists, Jews, agnostics, Buddhists and Christians are pulled together by the vision of man's ability to reason together; by man's ability to rise above his sectarian beliefs.[11]

Sterling McMurrin in *The Schools and the Challenge of Innovation*, says: "In our society, education concerns first the well-being of the individual pupil and student, his capabilities for a productive and happy life in which he can pursue an interesting and satisfying vocation."[12] This view of education ignores the origin and place of man, the relation between creation and Creator, and questions of absolute authority and morality.[13] Assuming that everyone is free and equal based a common human rationality, society attempts to meet both individual and societal needs in one "common" school system. The American way has been erected on the freedom to hold varying beliefs, ideas, ways of life. However, in a democracy where majority rules, those diverse perspectives have to be melted down to what is common among all men and women. Basic convictions are private and must be left behind during the week when everyone works together for the "common good." Schools are the instrument to educate citizens in this "common" way of life.

In 1951 the Educational Policies Commission of the N.E.A. presented a declaration on *Moral and Spiritual Values in the Public Schools*. It explained that "By moral and spiritual values we mean those values which, when applied to human behavior, exalt and refine life and bring it into accord with the standards of conduct that are approved in our democratic culture."[14] As a result, teachers and students must leave their basic beliefs about life and the world at home for fear of offending someone. The important questions about life cannot really be discussed because there are deep-rooted differences of opinion about these matters.

> Here is the old myth of the common core of religion at the heart of all religions. It is comparable to saying that we must hold to a respect for monarchy, fascism, naziism, communism, feudalism, republicanism and democracy and believe in the moral and spiritual values shared by all of them. It would be to affirm a belief in government as such as being moral, irrespective of its character. Religion as such can be true or false, good or bad, decadent or virile. *To affirm religion as such is to affirm the irrelevance of all moral and spiritual values*, and this is the true implication of this stand taken by the Educational Policies Commission.[15]

The school is forced to concentrate on issues which are non-debatable in order to further the concept of common ground.

When important matters are dealt with, the way to be non-controversial is to present a variety of viewpoints and allow the student to choose. The student soon realizes that it does not make much difference which he chooses. With no framework in which to decide and understand, no vision, and no direction, students lose their sense of commitment and meaning in life. Of course commitment, meaning, values, and purpose in life are all emphasized, but they are words without content. For in this view, content brings intolerance and discrimination. This is the religion of "commitment to non-commitment." The lowest common denominator is what is taught in the classroom.

> The antinomies, confusions and ambiguities such a policy causes in education are strikingly clear, for example, in so-called sex education. Since differing faith communities have differing conceptions of the nature of marriage, the state school has to leave open the question of the real nature of marriage. If it taught any one view it would be discriminating against those holding divergent views. But it must teach something. Consequently, in least-common-denominator fashion, under the guise of factuality and neutrality, the school teaches only the mechanics and techniques of sex. By default students are taught that sex is more or less all there is to marriage. The Christian view of marriage—that it is basically a relationship of fidelity, troth or love between husband and wife for life based on sexual union—cannot be taught.[16]

This illustration shows how a vision of life is expressed even in the school's curriculum and methodology. My own college sociology textbook offers a further illustration for our discussion.

In a section entitled "The Functions of Education," this "least common denominator" textbook examines the American educational system. Recognizing John Dewey as the most influential person in the history of American education, the author explains:

> To Dewey, *education* was synonymous with what we have called socialization; *schooling* was any formalized teaching or learning of particular academic skills. Thus schooling was only part of education and not necessarily the most important part. What *was*

important, if children were to become true citizens of
a democracy, was that they should learn to trust in
their own experience. And one of the things that their
experience should teach them was the value of cooperation, which Dewey saw as the basis of democracy. Here, he thought, was a chance for the school
—especially now that attendance was compulsory—
to take over where society had failed. It could provide a democratic community in which the individual
child could develop into a worthy citizen.[17]

Notice that the purpose of education for Dewey is to develop
the child into a worthy, democratic citizen who knows the
value of cooperation. Continuing, the author refers to an
N.E.A. report by the Commission of the Reorganization of
Secondary Education. The report lists the "seven major aims
of education," which are as follows:

1. health
2. command of fundamental processes
3. worthy home membership
4. vocation
5. citizenship
6. worthy use of leisure time
7. ethical character

The author adds that "These aims were to be realized through
'*common* courses for *all* in general education, *common* ex-
tracurricular activities, and the comprehensive high school' "
(emphasis ours).[18] Clearly, these aims do not conflict with the
democratic common denominator. The section concludes by
discussing "Conflicts in Goal Definition": "Because of their
different orientations, the various categories of participants
in the educational system seldom agree entirely on what the
schools should accomplish, or how." The controversies
themselves are in three categories: debates over purpose and
method, control, and "other." Using a Harris Poll we see these
results:

> Concerning the functioning of the school, 62 percent
> of parents believed that maintaining discipline
> should take priority over student self-inquiry; only 27
> percent of teachers agreed. On the question of
> whether homework requiring memorization was
> good and useful; 70 percent of parents said that it
> was, compared to only 46 percent of teachers . . .

According to this same poll, most teachers and principals "would agree that schools are not the place to foster controversy or to challenge prevailing standards," and most parents think that the schools "should keep children passive and disciplined, and provide them with the tools that lead to college and a job." Many students, on the other hand, are prepared to challenge "the system" both within and outside the school.[19]

Both parents and teachers avoid the significant issues, relegating them to the "other" category. Examples of the "other" conflicts include: "Who should be educated and what should be taught? What teaching methods should be used? Should education be general or specialized? Should it be predominantly humanistic or scientific?"[20] Answers to all of these questions and concerns about education would reflect particular visions of life. And notice that these "goal definitions" do not even include such questions as: What is the nature and destiny of man? Is there an absolute standard of right and wrong? What is the meaning of culture and history and of all our efforts and achievements? What is the highest goal of mankind? What does death mean? Does God exist? If He does, who is He? And what is the significance of the answers to these questions for the educating of our children? How should these answers affect our school design, our methodology, our curriculum?

These are not the kinds of questions American schools wrestle with, and yet these questions are basic to life. How we answer them determines how we understand who men and women are, the shape of their society, and their place and task in it. Educational decisions are made by adults who have a peculiar vision for life. That vision for life is impressed upon us and our children, and will be impressed upon our children's children.

What is our response as Christian students and parents? As servants of the Lord Jesus Christ can we offer ourselves and our children to be educated and trained in a view of life that does not instruct us in the way of the Lord? Here are four Christian responses to the call for obedience in the area of education from an essay by John A. Olthuis, entitled, "Towards Implementing the Vision of Christian Education."[21] Which of these is most like your view?

1. This view "is based on the conviction that the natural world (politics, education, business, the arts, and so on) is basically untouched by the fall into sin; so therefore, Christians and unbelievers have a common task to develop it, and young people from all faith communities (both Christian and atheist for example) should receive an identical education to prepare them to participate in an identical manner in building and developing the natural world. This educative process takes place in the public school. This view might well be labeled the 'sell-out' view, because it sells out certain areas of life to one or another variant of the humanist religion."

2. This position states "that the natural world is bad and irredeemable, so Christians can only go into it when it's necessary, such as for economic reasons, and when they do go into it, they can't change it; it's basically irredeemable, so the best they can do is hope to change some people in it. The school, therefore, must teach Christian ethics and standards of conduct to students so that they can change the world. This view may be labeled the 'sprinkling' view; sprinkling a little Christianity on top of a basically bad world will somehow make the bad world better through individual contributions, even though that world itself will not and cannot change."

3. This choice "is based on the conviction that the world is not only bad and irredeemable, but it is so bad that it has a negative influence on Christians and in particular on Christian young people. These young people must therefore be isolated from the world. This view may be called the 'hothouse' view, because it isolates and educates young people in an artificial manner."

4. "The fourth view is based on the conviction that the world and everything in it was affected both by the fall into sin and by the resurrection of Jesus Christ, and that Christians have a corporate responsibility to claim all areas of life for Jesus Christ. This view rejects the assumption that the world is good in itself, or bad and irredeemable, and holds that the Scriptures teach us the world was cast into sin by the fall, but the possibility for redemption is secured through the resurrection of Jesus Christ. Hence, the

Christian school must train the child in the total Kingdom perspective. This means training the child to do everything, including his politics and his business, in an integrally Christian manner."

One essential idea is common to the first three views and distinguishes them from the fourth, the idea that there are two realms in the universe. One realm is "sacred" and redeemable; the other is "secular" and unredeemable. The creation that God made is divided in half, with certain areas and concerns of life placed in the "upper" half, making these "spiritual" or "religious," while others belong to the "lower" half, which is deemed "worldly" or "non-religious." Supposedly, God is concerned only with the upper realm, which would include Heaven, theology, prayer, church, morals and meaning, and the soul. The lower realm consists of the earth; cultural activities such as politics, economics, the sciences, the arts, and education; work; the body; and public concerns, all of which have little or nothing to do with the upper realm. Of course, we all must live on the earth and be heavily involved in the things of the lower realm which include most of the time of our lives on this planet. Often the only time the two realms are united is when there is the possibility of being moral on the job or doing some "personal" evangelism at a social affair. The lower realm is usually considered to be neutral, or autonomous; and in these activities society is not directly responsible to God. Men and women make the Laws here, excluding the upper realm from their picture of the universe; the frame they use is too small for the picture. Their view of life, called "humanism," regards humans as supreme and autonomous beings in the universe. With their ability to reason (which distinguishes humans from the other animals on this planet), they decide everything about life—what defines life and death; what is right and wrong; what is society; what is good or bad for society.

This view differs sharply from what is revealed to us in the Scripture, and yet it is deeply embedded in our thinking and our society. Three of the views of education stated are attempts Christians have made to blend these two views of life together—two views which have conflicting purposes, goals, priorities, and visions for life. If a man or woman believes that God's Word is the Law for all life can he or she also believe that life is a matter of survival of the fittest in international politics, business, human relationships, and even education? Should not our "private" beliefs manifest themselves in these "public" areas of life and expose our heart commitments, giving witness to the God in whose service we should live and die?

Following are some excerpts from John Van Dyk's essay, "Building a Curriculum with the Kingdom Vision," which illustrate the influence which a view of life has on the curriculum of a school.[22] Three views are considered: a humanistic approach, a "dualistic" Christian view in which the Christian and the Humanist faiths are synthesized (a "common" effort at education?), and a Biblical vision.

1. *Humanistic Vision and Curriculum Model*

Let us examine, by way of example, the ideal and the vision that directs the typical North American secular school—whether on the elementary, secondary, or college level. Men, according to this humanistic vision, are rational products of a long evolutionary process. They are free, autonomous individuals whose challenge it is to gain ever more control of nature. And what is nature? No more than a world of matter and atoms functioning according to inherent natural laws. Men, meanwhile, direct their own destiny. They create their own social order according to their own rational insight. *They* decide what government, marriage, and economic activity shall be. As biological organisms, endowed with reason and certain basic needs, men decide what is to be considered good and what is to be considered bad. Such decisions, of course, are to be made democratically.

Now observe how this humanistic vision affects the curriculum. (1) First there are the natural sciences, designed to give the pupil some understanding of that factual world of matter run by natural law, from which he has developed, and over which he must gain technological control. (2) Then there are the social and behavioral sciences, designed to explain how men as rational beings order their society and are to order it in accordance with the ideal of a harmonious American democracy. (3) Then there must be the humanities, consisting of courses geared to give the student a sense of morality and a set of values, established by society. (4) Meanwhile, certain areas that don't quite fit into these three categories are subject to debate. For example, is history a social science or a "humanity"? There is less question, of course, about what history lessons should do; they are to show how civilization is on the way from an abominably primitive stage to a golden future of a warless, harmonious, perfectly democratic society.

2. "Dualistic" Christian Curriculum Model

Observe now how this type of curriculum has in structure and in content been adopted and adapted by Christian dualistic schools. The three divisions established by secular education remain basically unchanged. (1) The natural sciences by and large still examine simply a world of matter run by inherent natural law—except, of course, that this world of nature was created by God and is in some undefined way subject to his providence. (2) The social studies are taught in very much the same way as in the secular school, with stress on the ideal of American democracy as a way of life. The autonomous rational dignity of man, meanwhile, has been replaced somewhat by the concept of man made in the image of God. (3) The humanities continue to be designed to give the student a set of values and virtues. Often these virtues differ very little from those taught in the secular schools—the dignity of man, the need for honesty, punctuality, diligence, tolerance, patience, citizenship, etc. Added to the humanities section are the Bible courses, designed to give the pupil an added spiritual dimension. (4) History as well is commonly taught in Christian schools in very much the same way as in the secular school. Not that the Christian history teacher blatantly teaches that man will reach a golden future. He substitutes the concept of the "plan of God" for that idea, and that is good. At the same time, however, the understanding of the actual historical process itself remains very much the same as that of the secular history teacher. That historical process continues to be seen as a chain of events occuring in the context of cause and effect. As a result, often in history class the student learns no more than (a) the dates, (b) the causes, and (c) the results of historical events. Thus often the "plan of God" concept no more than baptizes what I believe to be an inherently secular understanding of historical events.

3. *The Biblical Kingdom Model* (In essence the Biblical Kingdom Vision hinges on three focus points; namely, (1) who God is, (2) who man is, and (3) what the world is.)

How, concretely now, does this Kingdom vision and task affect the curriculum? Here are just a few examples. First, the natural sciences cannot be taught as a mere body of knowledge which explains the universe as a cold world of matter, atoms, and inherent natural laws. Rather, natural science must explain the created order as structured and responding to God's Word of power. The effects of the concept of inherent natural law must be radically eliminated, a most difficult thing to do. Natural science, therefore, as well as technology, must be understood as a *cultural* activity, as an obedient or disobedient response to the will of the Lord. I might add, at this point, that Christian elementary schools often succeed much more in conveying the biblical concept of God's world to the children than the advanced levels of education. Much of this success, in fact, is rendered meaningless in junior high, high school, and college, where natural sciences once more are treated as so many independent and unrelated bodies of abstract facts.

Second, social sciences can no longer be taught as mere descriptions of what is actually taking place. Rather, the God-oriented norms and ordinances for the various societal structures such as state, family, marriage, school, labor, and industry must be clarified to the Christian student, so that in terms of these norms he will gain insight into the *de*formations that have taken place in our civilization. This, in turn, will enable him to join the throng of fellow-believers as a Kingdom citizen, struggling together with them for the *re*formation of what unbelief has distorted.

Third, "humanities" can no longer be courses whose function it is to instill a set of values and a sense of morality in pupils. "Humanities" will no longer be contrasted with natural sciences as value is contrasted with fact, since natural sciences themselves, as I indicated a moment ago, must be understood as cultural activity, and therefore as a response to what the Lord wants men to do. The Kingdom vision must guide again: how has the art, music, language, and literature of civilization been deformed by men who turned their backs on the Lord? How can we understand the nature of art and language and all the other fields so that these dimensions of God's world, too, can be reclaimed for Jesus Christ? Take art, for example. Day after day the Christian community is bombarded by the secular spirits in art, on TV, in magazines, on the billboards along the highway. All of this molds and forms us, and shapes us into the standard American consumer. Where is the Christian alternative? The Christian curriculum, therefore, must incorporate work in art in such a way that Kingdom citizens come out of our schools ready and able to do battle with the spirits, including those spirits that have gained control of the art forms of North America.

Fourth, history courses can no longer be taught as masses of events related in a context of cause and effect. Rather, history will be seen as man's response to God's call to be active in the world, to keep and to dress the garden. The various sequences of events, therefore, must be evaluated in terms of a biblically-directed understanding of God's will for cultural development. History courses must vividly highlight the antithesis between the children of light and the children of darkness. Historical studies must equip the Christian school graduate to understand the spirits of the age, their nature, their origin, and their effectiveness. In this way the Christian school graduate can take his place in the army of the Lord to combat the forces of secularism, humanism, pragmatism, dualism, individualism, and all other isms that are not of God and which now collectively have a death grip on North American education, politics, economics, art, and communications.

Can you see what an incredible difference a vision for life makes in the educational program of a school? Even the selection and arrangement of subject matter, the way in which it is taught, and the specific goals set are imbued with the decision maker's vision of life. Jesus said: "Let the little children come to me, and do not hinder them, for the kingdom of heaven belongs to such as these" (Matt. 19:14). Harro Van Brummelen points out: "We cannot determine the student's heart commitment, but we *can* structure the curriculum so that the faith that *is* present is fostered, and show what faith is and how it encompasses and directs our lives."[23] The ultimate goal in John Dewey's philosophy of education—that of developing the child into a dedicated democratic citizen whose highest value is cooperation—falls far short of God's command to teach our children His Law, that they might be equipped to live a completely Christian life in today's culture. Contrast Dewey's view with the following by Van Brummelen:

> Since the ultimate goal of Christian education is to equip the student to respond positively to God's calling in all areas of life, the curriculum must prepare our students for the tasks and responsibilities that he now faces and that lie ahead. He must learn to function in his own unique, responsible way in such things as showing Christian troth in marriage and the family; exercising his responsibility as a voter and citizen as well as in the world of work; using his God-given economic resources in a responsible way both personally and in business; helping to form a Christian mind with respect to concepts such as justice, freedom, sexuality, and the welfare state; appreciating the necessity of developing Christian approaches to art, music, the mass media, the use of leisure time; having a Christian consciousness with respect to the poor, the sick, the aged, the emotionally ill, and minority groups. For all this the student must have an understanding of the biblical norms for life as well as of the underlying religious motives of our culture.[24]

Thinking people are concerned about the current crisis in education; they recognize the fact that our formal educational systems have a tremendous influence on the student's thoughts and beliefs—as much influence as music, television, and movies. Of course there are many more examples of how different visions for life affect our culture and of how a Christian view of life can be demonstrated in our daily activities. But before we leave our classroom to look around at some of these, let us hear again what Moses said: "See, I have taught you decrees and laws as the Lord my God commanded me . . . Teach them to your children and to their children after them."

Notes

1. Calvin Seerveld, *Rainbows for the Fallen World: Aesthetic Life and Artistic Task* (Toronto: Tuppence Press, 1980), p. 32.
2. Seerveld, *Rainbows for the Fallen World: Aesthetic Life and Artistic Task*, p. 33.
3. Harry Blamires, *The Christian Mind: How Should a Christian Think?* (Ann Arbor: Servant Books, 1978), p. 34.
4. Calvin Seerveld, *Cultural Objectives for the Christian Teacher* (Palos Heights, IL: Trinity College), p. 14.
5. D.B. Knox, "Righteousness," *The New Bible Dictionary*, 1979 ed., ed. J.D. Douglas et al. (Grand Rapids: William B. Eerdmans Publishing Company, 1962), p. 1097. It is understood here, that according to God's standard, our own righteousness is insufficient for salvation.
6. Harry M. Kuitert, *Signals from the Bible*, trans. Lewis B. Smedes (Grand Rapids: William B. Eerdmans Publishing Company, 1972), pp. 36-37.
7. D. Bruce Lockerbie, *The Timeless Moment: Creativity and the Christian Faith* (Westchester, IL: Cornerstone Books, 1980), pp. 52-53.
8. Hendrik Hart, "Cultus and Covenant," in *Will All the King's Men . . .: Out of Concern for the Church, Phase II* (Toronto: Wedge Publishing Foundation, 1972), pp. 34-35.
9. John C. VanderStelt, "The Struggle for Christian Education in Western History," in *To Prod the "Slumbering Giant": Crisis, Commitment, and Christian Education* (Toronto: Wedge Publishing Foundation, 1972), pp. 45-46.
10. N.E.A., *The Unique Function of Education in American Democracy*, 1937, pp. 71-72.
11. John A. Olthuis, "Hidden Invaders of Our Homes," in *Hope for the Family* (Toronto: Wedge Publishing Foundation, 1971), pp. 26-27.
12. Sterling McMurrin, "Innovation and the Purposes of Education," in *The Schools and the Challenge of Innovation*, H. Thomas James et al. (New York: McGraw-Hill Book Company, 1969), p. 7.
13. John Vriend, "No Neutral Ground: Why I'm Committed to Christian Education," in *To Prod the "Slumbering Giant": Crisis, Commitment, and Christian Education* (Toronto: Wedge Publishing Foundation, 1972), p. 6.
14. N.E.A., *Moral and Spiritual Values in the Public Schools*, 1951, p. 3.

15. Rousas J. Rushdoony, *Intellectual Schizophrenia: Culture, Crisis and Education* (New Jersey: Presbyterian and Reformed Publishing Company, 1978), p. 63.

16. James H. Olthuis, "To Prod the 'Slumbering Giant,' " in *To Prod the "Slumbering Giant": Crisis, Commitment and Christian Education* (Toronto: Wedge Publishing Foundation, 1972), p. 22.

17. Melvin L. DeFleur, William V. D'Antonio, and Lois B. De Fleur, *Sociology: Human Society* (Glenview, IL: Scott, Foresman and Company, 1973, 1971), p. 566.

18. DeFleur et al., p. 567.

19. DeFleur et al., p. 569.

20. DeFleur et al., p. 572.

21. John A. Olthuis, "Towards Implementing the Vision of Christian Education," in *To Prod the "Slumbering Giant": Crisis, Commitment, and Christian Education* (Toronto: Wedge Publishing Foundation, 1972), pp. 146-148.

22. John Van Dyk, "Building a Curriculum with the Kingdom Vision," in *To Prod the "Slumbering Giant": Crisis, Commitment, and Christian Education* (Toronto: Wedge Publishing Foundation, 1972), pp. 99-106.

23. Harro Van Brummelen, "Towards a Radical Break with the Public School Curriculum," in *To Prod the "Slumbering Giant": Crisis, Commitment, and Christian Education* (Toronto: Wedge Publishing Foundation, 1972), pp. 72-73.

24. Van Brummelen, p. 81.

Chapter 6

Daily Obedience in the Activities of Life—II

Fix These Words in Your Hearts and Minds

> Tumble out of bed and stumble to the kitchen
> Pour myself a cup of ambition
> Yawn and stretch and try to come to life
> Jump in the shower and the blood starts pumping
> Out on the street the traffic starts jumping
> With folks like me on the job from nine to five
>
> Working nine to five
> What a way to make a living
> Barely getting by
> It's all taking and no giving
> They just use your mind
> And they never give you credit
> It's enough to drive you crazy if you let it
>
> They let you dream just to watch them shatter
> You're just a step on the boss man's ladder
> But you got dreams they'll never take away
> In the same boat with a lot of your friends
> Waiting for the day your ship will come in
> Then the tide's going to turn
> And it's all going to roll your way

Dolly Parton sang this song—the theme from the movie *9 to 5*. Consider, too, a line from *Morning Train*, sung by Sheena Easton: "(my baby) works all day to earn his pay, so we can play all night." Are these healthy views of work? What drives people to put up with the 9 to 5 grind? "In this highly competitive world, Paine-Webber believes the quality of life just

81

might depend on the quality of your investments." And so, motivated by dreams, retirement plans, or the hope of affluence, and appeased by playing at night and on weekends, we are exhorted in our culture to work harder than good sense would allow at jobs that offer no lasting satisfaction.

Shifts in education reflect cultural attitudes regarding work. It used to be that schools emphasized a broad spectrum of academic requirements to prepare a person for living in the world. Today education emphasizes the technical skills necessary to get a job. Trade and technical schools enrollments are growing (a 15% increase from the 1980-81 to the 1981-82 school years). Henry R. Herzing, president of the National Association of Trade and Technical Schools, captures the spirit of the times when he aserts: "Our single mission is to train people in the shortest amount of time for the best possible job . . . After all, a good job is part of the good life. Helping students get ready for the job is our goal."[1] Even general academic institutions have shifted emphases from liberal arts departments to business and technical majors.

Sociologist Arthur Levine has studied and identified some of the characteristics of contemporary college and university students which contribute to this shifting emphasis. They are "looking out for number one," with "an almost singleminded concern for material success." Levine demonstrates that this "MEism" "permeates all aspects of the undergraduate world, from politics to education to social life to the future that students envision." Students throughout North America today "are more career-oriented and more competitive."[2] He shows that students of the sixties were seeking personal fulfillment, but that students of the eighties seek material success instead. He longs to convince them that there is more to life.[3] Educational experts decry the shift to technical emphases and meaningless work to pay the bills for "the good life."

In its own style, *Rolling Stone* magazine identifies these same shifting attitudes. In an article entitled, "How to Get a Good Job," T.J. O'Rourke states:

> The definition of a good job has evolved in the last fifteen years. In a sixties good job, you changed the system while realizing your own potential as a person. In a seventies good job, you discovered the best way to change the system was by becoming successful within it while realizing your own potential in a

leisure context. This led to the eighties good job, where you make lots of money and get to screw off.[4]

This same attitude is exposed in current beer commercials. In the seventies it was "Weekends were made for Michelob!" The work-week was endured for the rewards of the weekend. However, the slogan in the eighties is "Put a little Weekend in your Week!" Since pleasure is the reward, why wait? The meaninglessness of work is everywhere: popular music, investment commercials, beer commercials, and our educational system foster this attitude of working for the sake of material benefits. If you can make "lots of money," no matter what you have to do, you can then buy the good life.

Does the Christian community cry out against these attitudes? There is certainly no cry that can be heard above the noise of our culture. In fact, in one way or another, most Christians find themselves in the very same rat-race. Perhaps the seriousness of the problem can be highlighted by the following illustration:

As I looked around the convention floor, I was struck with the clean, shining exteriors of the people who were there at the Good Soap and Household Sales Program.

I decided to ask those who were to be honored for their high sales volumes, about their jobs. Several who were Christians were particularly helpful. When I asked them how they incorporated their faith and their jobs, four answered in this way:

1. "I can sell anything.

"I guess that's just my gift. I'm performing a service, providing people with what they want . . . Pollution? Unfair marketing? If there were anything wrong with it, the government wouldn't let me do it. Hey, I sell good products and at reasonable prices. What else could you ask for? Why shouldn't I succeed?!"

2. "I'm a people person.

"Selling brings me in contact with people all over the community. Occasionally they ask me why I'm always so positive and smile all the time. I have a chance to tell them about my walk with the Lord.

"People say that they really enjoy buying from me because I make them so happy."

3. "I've made it to the top, but discovered that none of these things count for eternity.

"I'm getting my award tonight and I'm quitting because there are important things to do for God. Next month I start at the Bible College to use my skills to sell Jesus."

4. "I'm very selective about what I sell.

"Some of the products in our line are pure hype. I avoid those and concentrate on the products that people need and find helpful. Often I feel that I'm not the most popular salesperson with the company because of the time I spend with families, helping them figure out their needs and the best buys for their money. My primary concern isn't the items with the highest commission, nor pushing some of the high mark-up 'specials.'

"God has endowed me with the ability to do sales, but I have to be discerning as to what is consistent with God's intention. In this way I feel I better serve my customers. It's like loving my neighbor!"

These four views suggest different ways that Christians can look at vocation. The first fails to take into account the reality of sin in the world, whether it be sin in one's own life (the salesperson's greed), the company (making and promoting needless or harmful items), the government (special interest groups pressuring for "their products" to be allowed on the market, despite questions), or the customer (people often want things they don't need or things that would be harmful to them). Should we not do our work with a constant awareness of the sin within and around us, if we desire to serve Christ there?

The second salesperson typifies the "missionary mentality." This person might well say, "It doesn't matter what I do as long as I witness for Jesus in the process!" This attitude divorces the "sacred" things from the everyday "secular" things. Such people fail to see the continuity between their personal and public lives, between their faith and their works.

The third salesperson is the "escapist." This person has tried to be consistent in everyday life and has experienced difficulty doing so. Rather than continue to take the hard knocks, he has chosen to withdraw into the "community of the redeemed," to try to avoid the struggle of living in an imperfect world. However, we need to see the Church as a place of refreshment from which to be sent out, not as a castle in which to be isolated.

The fourth response demonstrates a healthy understanding of vocation. Realizing the reality of sin, this person is cautious about what is sold and how people are "convinced" to buy it. He takes time to investigate, and if the product is found to be useless or harmful, he will not sell it. He realizes that God has given a responsibility to the employer as well as to the customers, and he takes both seriously. This means that at times he challenges the product line promoted by the company and at times challenges the desires of the customers. He realizes the abilities and gifts that God has given and seeks to use those abilities and gifts in a way that honors God and demonstrates Christian concern for one's neighbor.[5]

The fourth salesperson exemplifies a person who has a good understanding of his or her vocation as a Christian. Realizing that one does not have to work in the church to pursue a Christian vocation, he or she seeks to use God-given talents to cultivate the creation which God has made good. A person is still responsible to evangelize and to serve the Church, but this need not be confused with occupation. A Christian is one whose vocation involves developing the potential which God put in the creation—working out the third stage of creation (see p. 18) as well as countering the effects of sin (see p. 52). Our vocation is Christian not because of our field, occupational interest, or specific task, but because of how we make basic decisions and do our work as Christians in our particular situation.

In their lives and vocations, all Christians must proclaim the Lord they serve. In addition, they have a responsibility to share the Good News of redemption in Christ with those around them who fail to acknowledge His Lordship. Co-workers, classmates, clients, neighbors and everyone we know, need to hear the message of salvation. It would be counterproductive to have our vocations point to the Lord we serve without telling people who that Lord is. Christian vocations and the Gospel message go hand in hand.

A vocation is "Christian" if it permits an individual to use the gifts that God has given him or her to further truth, justice, mercy, and love. Some jobs cannot be Christian: In our community, a local television station once highlighted an "actress" who used her strip-tease act to witness for Christ. That is a contradiction in terms, for she violates her own personhood to do evangelism. Christians can do jobs in an unChristian way, for example, the Christian politician who lets his or her political ideology override Christian convictions. Yet we are called to live out our lives as Christians in our devotional lives, in our family lives, our work-a-day lives, and our leisure. Work should allow men and women to assist and serve, to care and show mercy, and to express themselves creatively and with grace. When the love and law of God is fixed in our hearts and minds, this becomes our inclination; great things will then result in our lives and in our world.

When You Get Up

For most Americans, "getting up" is associated with an alarm clock, a shower, a brief news and weather report, and a trip to work to "make a living," whether it be in an office or a steel mill. In the midst of economic tensions, many breathe a sigh of relief that they can keep a roof over their heads and food on their tables. Scarcity has taken on new meaning. Scarcity of resources, energy, and clean air have accompanied unemployment and spiraling inflation. With the oil crisis, Americans became aware of the influence of the international situation on our everyday economics. Bob Goudzwaard paints a vivid portrait of this state of affairs:

> Something is rotten in our western society. We know it, we see it all around us, yet we don't know what to do about it. Instead of activating us, the situation seems to paralyze us. A society that has chosen to live an autonomous (i.e. self-governing) life is now staggering toward its autonomous death. And such a death can only make us feel quite helpless.
>
> Am I too gloomy, too pessimistic? I don't think so. In our cities the garbage trucks are busily picking up the leftovers of our consuming society. They are gathering the remnants of our half-eaten cakes and cream tarts. And at this very moment the refuse carts in Bombay and Ethiopia are collecting the bodies of men, women, and children who died last night in the streets and fields of hunger and misery.[6]

However, it is not just the contrast between Western Society and the Third World that deserves our attention. Conditions in our own society must also be scrutinized. Goudzwaard continues:

> In our own "great" society thousands of workers are forced to perform monotonous, mind-killing tasks only to serve the prefabricated, dehumanized needs of our modern leisure activities. We see the dead fish and the darkening shadows in our streams

and lakes, results of the endless and meaningless hunt for new detergents and chemicals. We witness costly preparations for future space flights, but little if any preparation for the future of America's black youths. The young make their hopeless protest against this repressive/tolerant technocratic society in which nonsense consumption is a national duty and in which increased production has become a self-legitimating issue. At the same time other young people try to escape the one-dimensional consumer society by turning themselves into drug-dreaming, zero-dimensional consuming animals. The riots, campus fights, and demonstrations of the sixties were, I believe, only the partial eruptions of a much greater, more explosive volcano underneath.

How could we have let things go this far? What is at the root of all these destructive developments, these seriously unbalanced situations in our rationally balanced society? And what should our position, our Christian attitude, be in such a world? Isn't everything we do, including all our labour, a confirmation of the very direction of that society, a further establishing of the establishment, a compromise with what we reject? Would it not be better for Christians simply to abandon the whole system and escape from it? These are serious questions, and our answers had better be serious as well.[7]

For most, to be Christians in economic life means living the way other Americans do, with the addition of being honest and witnessing on the job, avoiding sexual involvement with co-workers, praying over difficult decisions, and giving a percentage of one's gross income to the Church. Aside from these addendums, Christians tend to "believe" politicians, industrial leaders, and technical scientific experts when they speak about our economic problems and their solutions. Have we gone too far in our technological and economic expansion? According to our society's leaders, the exact opposite is true. They would have us believe that more technology will solve the problems we face in these days. For instance, they imply that pollution or nuclear waste problems caused by technological development will be eliminated painlessly by further technological development. Here we see a societal confession, a statement of faith, "that things would get better and better through the advance of modern technology within the framework of a growing free market production."[8] This is nothing less than a trusting belief that this way of life is the path to Life, Health, and Happiness for the people who follow it. It is a faith that our lives will be fulfilled through technology and economic growth.

However, once on this path, how do we deal with the loneliness which has no economic or technological solution? Will my daughter have a healthy identity if she wears expensive designer blue jeans to school? Will my work be fulfilling if I can afford expensive weekend entertainment? Will a woman find happiness as mother and wife if she gets a microwave oven for Christmas? Will old people never feel lonely again if we give them all color televisions? Is my income really the measure of my ability and accomplishment? Is my worth as a human being purely economic? If not, then why are wealthy people treated with greater respect than the poor? Why are engineers more valued in our society than poets? Is it because technical experts are more essential to reaching our societal goals than poets? What are these goals?

This book has maintained adamantly that no dimension of life is of itself evil or demonic. All aspects of life are given by God as a part of His creation and are to be developed in service. How, then, are Christians to demonstrate their faith in their economic life? We cannot deny that our society exhibits a strong belief in economic development as the source of both personal and societal happiness. As the apostle Paul informs us in his letter to the Romans, humans are transformed into the image of the god or gods that they serve (Rom. 1:18ff). The economic direction of western society is a religious one—a confession of faith involving a view of man and the world.[9]

Christians should recognize that the problem lies not with the economic structure itself, but lies, rather, in the hearts of men and women. Remember the proverb: "Above all else, guard your heart, for it is the wellspring of life" (4:23). Economic life is a manifestation of what men and women believe; it is a working out of faith—faith in God or faith in idols. Christians can neither try to escape from the powerful economic structure, nor compromise with its view of life.

To begin to redirect our economic thinking and acting, we move beyond criticizing our present situation and, in the light of Scripture, try to think about our work as if it were to complete the redemptive work of Christ. On what does our happiness as Christians depend? Is our work a "negative" and the possession of goods a "positive"? Quite the opposite. As we saw in the opening chapters of Genesis, men and women are to be cultivators, caretakers in God's world: "The Lord God took the man and put him in the Garden of Eden to work it and take care of it" (Gen. 2:15). Men and women are to be responsible in that they are to respond to the Lord of this creation: "The earth is the Lord's, and everything in it, the world and all who live in it: (Ps. 24:1). Humankind carries the obligation to carry out God's Word on the earth. Economic life, too, must be developed and cultivated, but it can never be separated from its purpose to serve God and neighbor. By way of an illustration, a man might cultivate a tree in God's creation by fashioning a bow and arrows from the wood. The man might then use the bow and arrows to protect his family from a wild beast or to hunt food. This is his stewardly response to God in cultivating the potential that lies in a tree He has made. On another occasion, in anger he might use the same bow and arrows to murder his neighbor. Again, this is a response, an answer to God in his "taking care of" the things God owns and has entrusted to him. The tree in itself is good and loaded with potential, which humans direct for good or evil. Economics, too, is filled with potential to serve God and neighbor, to demonstrate God's wisdom and glory in His creation. However, in the hands of those who serve false gods, economics can destroy and make life miserable for people.

Therefore, we see that our work and our economic life is filled with potential "witness" about our God. Consider the sabbatical system in the Mosaic society which allowed rest for the land and reconciliation for people. Those who were so far in debt that they had to sell themselves and their families into indentured service could hope and eventually find redemption when the year of Jubilee cancelled their debts and liberated them from service (see Lev. 25). Here is an economic system which demonstrates God's wisdom and glory. Modeled on reconciliation, it illustrates in economic life the redemption God provides through His Son.

Similarly, Scripture often cautions against the accumulation of wealth, which is very highly valued in our society. We are warned often that one can easily be duped by a desire to become rich: "Whoever trusts in his riches will fall, but the righteous will thrive like a green leaf" (Prov. 11:28); ". . . though your riches increase, do not set your heart on them" (Ps. 62:10b); "Again I tell you, it is easier for a camel to go through the eye of a needle than for a rich man to enter the kingdom of God" (Matt. 19:24). The widow's "two very small copper coins, worth only a fraction of a penny," in God's eyes outweigh the large amounts of money given by the rich to the temple treasure. Goudzwaard points out that:

> In the Christian community something has to become visible of the holiness and the harmony of the economics of the Kingdom of God. A basic rule of that Kingdom is that happiness lies more in giving than receiving, that a man can become rich in Christ by giving away his treasures. In that community social, economic, and racial differences, rather than causing separation, have to intensify genuine communion and solidarity, transforming that community into a place of real and substantial healing for all who are hurt and broken by an idolatrous culture.[10]

Where are the real points of happiness in our lives? What do we trust? Which god do we follow in the economic activities of our lives? Pondering these questions may help us reevaluate or even restructure our economic priorities to conform to the Lord's calling.

Do you see how economic decisions demonstrate what lies in people's hearts? There are no miracle cures for our ailing economic condition. Christians must consider carefully what for them constitutes obedient economic living. Those of us who say, "Trust in God, but tie up your camel," must ask ourselves where our trust lies—in God or the rope. I return to Bob Goudzwaard:

> I am inclined to say that we have to start from the beginning and open up our lives. However, we should not believe that we ourselves can reorient everything that is going on in this world as a result of following gods that have betrayed us. We should trust our Savior, but that trust also has a deep meaning for our economic life. It does not bring with it a full program for the total reorientation of the world, but asks instead for signposts of the kingdom. We are to erect signposts that demonstrate in this world that our orientation point lies in Christ, that he is the beginning and the end of economic life. He is our steward, the source of our happiness. If Christ becomes the starting point in our life, he will bring with him a different lifestyle. That is a signpost in a culture.[11]

There is such a signpost in the City of Pittsburgh.

Write Them on Your Gates

Dwelling House Savings and Loan Association is located on a corner in the Hill District, an inner city area of Pittsburgh, Pennsylvania. Under the leadership of Robert R. Lavelle, executive vice president, it has grown from a savings base in the late fifties of less than $500,000 to more than $7,000,000 currently. A promotional brochure explains the enterprise in this way:

> Most banks are in business to lend at the highest possible interest with the lowest possible risk. Unfortunately, this means that the poor, the black, and other minorities rarely receive mortgage money to buy and own their own homes. Precisely because they're poor and disadvantaged they involve higher financial risk, moreover, they're least likely to pay high interest.
>
> Dwelling House attempts to reverse the traditional banking rule—by lending to people who may not be "good risks," at the lowest practical interest rate. Our goal is to approach people with respect and through encouragement and patient financial counseling, to help them become *good* risks.
>
> This follows God's command to serve the poor and the needy. In addition, it helps build up disadvantaged communities—because home ownership leads to increased civic involvement, increased political pressure for adequate community services like police and fire protection, and increased incentive for business to locate in the area. When the residents of a community become owners of a community, they become directly responsible for property taxes and the educational system these taxes support."[12]

Many of the loans that Dwelling House makes are to people with little ability to make a normal down payment. A private corporation, Dwelling House helps significantly in community development and revitalization. It can do this because of very *low operating costs* (little advertising expense and the "missionary" wages of the executives), by avoiding loan defaults through *personal financial counseling* (whole families are counselled about their responsibility for the mortgage), and by *not offering the popular high-interest certificates of deposit* (because these would force loan rates up

beyond the level affordable by the poor and, further, such certificates are primary contributors to the inflationary spiral
which affect the poor most profoundly).

Dwelling House is a sound business venture which exemplifies the grace of God in its operations. Although extraordinary in its practices (government inspectors have ex-
claimed that the Dwelling House practices are impossible),
the success of this venture is demonstrated by increasing net
worth each year.

In addition, Lavelle and his co-workers are demonstrating
that a black business in the Hill District can be not only
legitimate but also profitable and helpful for the community.
Despite insurance problems, Lavelle insists on big windows
so that the neighborhood kids can see a good model and infer
that they are trusted. He takes only a minimal salary and
keeps his own IRA (retirement account) in a Dwelling House
account at regular passbook rates (the highest rate of return
Dwelling House provides). In his leadership at Dwelling
House, as well as in his own real estate business, Lavelle has
taken seriously the fact that "The earth is the Lord's and
everything in it" (Ps. 24:1).

Dwelling House has demonstrated that a successful
business is one that serves the community, "meeting people's
needs," and justifies its profit as such, rather than as the
primary objective of the business venture.

When You Walk Along the Road

If people expect technical science and economic growth
to be the gods who will lead them through the wilderness to a
world of happiness and fulfillment, this will affect other areas
of life. Why is the cinema the number one place to take a date?
Why is most living room furniture arranged in a semi-circle
around the television set, as though it were a primary source
of knowledge? How is television programing determined?
What makes popular music popular? What is a healthy style
for family life—one that breeds security, freedom, and a
strong sense of identity in the Lord?

In an essay entitled "Thoughts on Leisure," Miki Beldman
explains that in our society "Success and meaning are
measured in productivity, rewarded by money. Being,
creativity, and recreation are of less value. Leisure has
become primarily that time in which we recuperate from the
tiredness, monotony, and tension created by our work—a
renewal and a refreshment period."[13] Sound familiar? In our

productivity-oriented culture leisure time serves the needs of economic growth. Rather than offering all of life to the Lord, we allow certain areas of life to exist for the sake of other, high priority areas. Everything is subordinated to our goal of complete fulfillment through technical and economic growth. On the other hand, many Americans regard leisure as their chief end, and subordinate much in their lives, even their work, to it. Thus, all the various aspects of life are not opened up, developed, and cultivated, for their own sakes within the creation.

For example, what makes a popular song or a movie a "good" artistic endeavor? The answer is predictable: "technical" excellence and "economic" success. No song wins a Grammy Award for its thematic content; the Academy Awards Committee does not have as one of its criteria the religious thrust of the film—the view of God, man, and the world as demonstrated by choice of plot, characterization, and the director's understanding of life. Neither does it matter whether the composer, the performer, the actor, the director, or the producing company believes what they are saying in their artistic "productions" (which is itself an economic term). Entertainment falls far short of response to the God who has given us the gift of aesthetic life. Instead of viewing the popular arts as another possible avenue of service to God, our society reduces them to technological and economic objects, becoming enslaved by audience size, box office receipts, and consumer desires.

Understand, however, that this does not mean that television programing should include "Christian" soap operas in which the "Christian" family has fewer problems than the non-believers across the street. Nor does it mean that "Christian" music includes born-again refrain, or that "Christian" films always end with the searching hero becoming a true believer. We cannot take the scope of the life God has given us and reduce it to a few experiences which we consider "Christian." Christian artistic endeavors—whether they be in film, dance, music, television programing, painting, or literature—should illustrate scriptural understandings of life. A one-hour television program might show the daily life of a man who owes his life to the company store. His routine nine-to-five day ends with an after-dinner drink, his slippers, and the newspaper. In the background the TV set blares while his children play games or do homework. His wife finishes the dishes and joins him for a series of half-hour sitcoms before retiring to the bedroom. His sex life is dull compared to his pornographic magazines and his row house on Maple Street is small and shabby next to the houses owned by the three-piece-suited businessmen who manage the steel mill. But he must keep on working and fighting for higher wages and more benefits in order to find true happiness and fulfillment.

Do you see how this might artistically demonstrate, from a Christian perspective, how bankrupt his way of life is? This television program would not directly "say" so; it would show it. Now consider a program in which union workers struggle for more humane work methods and production techniques. They try to reduce the mindlessness of the assembly line and are willing to give up significant wage increases to see this happen. As the workers gain more responsibility in their work, their own self-image improves, labor/management disputes are reduced, and family life begins to improve. With a healthier view of life, they develop relationships with their neighbors, no longer feeling that they have to keep up with them to be successful. They start to say that life is good and worth living and learning about, and whoever put life together this way was a creative genius. Both of these television programs demonstrate a Christian view of life. The first exposes the effects of sin and the second illustrates the renewal that is possible through Christ.

If our activity in the popular arts is done in response to God and exposes the reality of sin in our culture while pointing the way to reconciliation, then many people will want to follow Him and live for Him. Of course, technical excellence is very important in any artistic endeavor and has much to do with its effectiveness. But equally important is the religious thrust of the work—what view of life does it demonstrate? Are men and women evolutionary animals who live in a survival-of-the-fittest world? Is there room for God in the world which this artistic production creates? Is there room for right and wrong? These kinds of questions help us uncover the vision of life art presents.

Talk About Them When You Sit at Home

Dr. Calvin Seerveld makes a point of saying that "An obedient aesthetic life is a matter of sanctification and not exactly a matter of heaven or hell."[14] We know that salvation is by God's grace only, not by any works we perform. Still, Jesus came that we might have life and have it completely. If all of life is a matter of responsible service to God, it follows that ignoring some aspects will undercut the health and wholeness of other aspects. Here we are discussing our response to God in daily aesthetic life. Style, taste, dress, home decorating, and language are examples of daily aesthetic life; our experience of film, music, and literature deepens our daily aesthetic experience.

God calls us to be understanding, sensitive, imaginative, sociable, honest, just, reliable, and communicative. We must realize that in everything we do—our thinking, our speaking, our acting—we represent Christ. With everything that we do, we are saying, "Neighbor, this is how I believe it should be done," whether it is an economic decision, the way we address our spouse and children both privately and in public, or the furniture we choose for our homes. There is a certain style to our living that betrays in whose service we live. Consider the following examples of style in family life.

> There is a family whose conversation is laced with references to such topics as the stock market, what's playing in London and New York, why the current political trouble spot materialized, and myriad interesting facts like the stage of rock sedimentation before Christ and the population of Tokyo. A visit with them is an amazing experience. Meals are on a pick-up basis except in the evening at seven o'clock, when it's a fairly formal dinner. You drink coffee out of pretty cups after dessert in the sitting room. Everybody has a responsible, industrious kind of job, but takes time to do sport or play bridge. Each one has opinions, but is polite. One is very cordial but a little reserved; there's always the breathing space of detachment in one's interest and commitments. The style as a whole is one of cultivated discretion. The roles of a classically educated gentleman and a woman of intelligent taste, aware of what's going on in the world, color all they do as a family. It's the style of their family way of life.

> There is another family whose middle-sized kitchen is the room of the house. Married children and their offspring gather there with the parents after the morning church service on Sunday, without fail, for coffee. They are an openhearted folk, gregarious and hospitable, somewhat impulsive, unadorned, always busy during the week at good tasks. Meals are straightforward—potatoes, gravy, vegetable, and a little piece of meat. Each one tends to be rather blunt,

no-offense, and has exaggerated loyalties to a base-
ball or hockey team. Although one's real feelings are
kept rather private, TV has largely replaced reading,
except for the Bible. There's a kind of matter-of-fact,
wholesome, take-for-granted, homespun style to the
family life. To do an honest day's work—to earn your
keep and a good night's sleep—is the style of their
routine.[15]

Both of these families affirm biblical possibilities for life-
styles in different societal settings. Obviously, there is no one
right style for all families in all ages to adopt. Yet here is a
discernible, subtle quality to the complexion of a family's life
which can be identified. Family life-style and home decor illustrate what people believe about life and the world.
Reflected in the very style of living is the family's view of
itself: what kind of responsibility does each member hold in
the family; what is important for discussion at dinner; what
do meals say about their view of world, national, and local affairs; how is family life affected by work or school? Life-style,
too, is our responsibility as stewards on the earth before the
Lord.

Similar questions can be raised about the way we speak,
the way we use God's gift of language. Do we demonstrate in
our conversation the wisdom and glory of God, with a
substantial use of words, a grasp of humor and metaphor, and
keen ears for hearing what our neighbors "really" mean when
they talk with us? Or do we merely wrap God's gift of
language in a package of "morality," with fancy paper that
contains no off-color jokes or local gossip? Is our conversation Christian only when we discuss the Bible and church activities or attempt evangelism? Shouldn't we be learning and
developing our manner of speech and style of persuasion, to
communicate better a Christian understanding of the political
and economic issues at stake in the next election; to articulate
a biblical view of discipline and curriculum at the school
board meeting; and to expose the religious direction of the
current film at the local theater? Language, then, is not simply a matter of knowing grammar. It is an integral part of
human experience. Through language we understand and
communicate the disruptive effects of sin on the personal and
communal life God has given us. Language points to the way
of redemption for all of life.

From this same perspective, what is our responsibility
before the Lord in the way we dress? Does clothing merely

keep us warm, or does it refurbish our lost glory as humans created in the image of God? If the latter is true, then our style of dress becomes another way to serve God.

> We are called to be dressed in ways that set off the color of our skin, the demeanor of our person, the lineaments of a homely face, the curves of our bodily sexuality, the dedication of our lives, the shape and strength of shoulder, arm, or leg, that will not arrest attention prizing itself, but reflect that you are corporeally a good-looking, godly man or boy, and a glorious girl or woman of God.[16]

It seems that most of us wear the kind of clothes we can afford and those that will allow us to fit into our social class. Is that responding to the Lord? Should our clothes put us on display, saying, "Look at me!" or should "the garments remain allusively functional, soft-pedaling their enrichment"[17] of a person's corporeal presence?

What about the neighborhood in which we live? Does a religious view of life determine the planning and laying out of a city? James Rouse, a nationally recognized expert on urban problems and a brilliant urban developer, says, "The only legitimate purpose of a city is to provide for the life and growth of its people."[18] The kind of life and the direction of that growth, then, are shaped, at least in part, by city planners. Rouse illustrates the effects of a city plan on the life of its people:

> Suburban sprawl stretches out the distances people must travel to work, to shop, to worship, to play. It fails to relate these activities in ways that strengthen each other, and thus it suppresses values that orderly relationships and concentration of uses would stimulate. Sprawl is inhuman. It is anti-human.[19]

All of life's activities can be done in responsible service to God, demonstrating His love and design for life—even city planning. Deeds which reflect false idols are bound to distort and fragment life, bringing sinful misery into the lives of people and their society. As Christians we must realize that not a moment of life is neutral—all activity is a matter of faith and service. All of us have the responsibility to continue to work out our salvation "with fear and trembling," for it is God who works in us "to will and to act according to his good purpose" (Phil. 2:12b, 13). We must be constantly investigating our activity at work, at play, at home, in political situations, in our marriages, in our schools, in our home decorating, and even in our landscaping, to distinguish the influence of the spirits of darkness from the Holy Spirit of God.

Not Just Idle Words

> When Moses finished reciting all these words to all Israel, he said to them, "Take to heart all the words I have solemnly declared to you this day, so that you may command your children to obey carefully all the words of this law. They are not just idle words for you—they are your life. By them you will live long in the land you are crossing the Jordan to possess" (Deut. 32:45-47).

To deny that all of life is service to God is to reduce God's Law to idle words—words void of meaning for our lives today. Is God's arm too short to give us direction and purpose for all of our activities? Would He abandon us in the marketplace, leave us with our frustration? Of course not.

Like the psalmist, we must all pray to the Lord:

> Your word is a lamp to my feet
>   and a light for my path.
> I have taken an oath and confirmed it,
>   that I will follow your righteous laws
>   (Ps. 119:105, 106).

Loving, obedient service, our grateful response to God, is what pleases the Lord. Living Christianly is the freedom to live life for God's sake, freed from the shackles of sin, free to respond in obedience to what God says about life.

> According to the Bible, the Kingdom of God is not a matter of doing what you know is permissible or of refraining from certain prescribed acts, but is the presence of right doing, peacemaking and joy, thanks to the Holy Spirit; women and men who do not trample on the conscience of those who are weak believers, but build up other persons, fill out their discipleship, and are contagious with an expectant gladness to be alive in God's world. Such women and men are serving Christ says the Bible, making God happy and passing the scrutiny of observant people.[20]

All of life can be touched by the glory of the Lord, saturated with God's presence, thus giving evidence of the goodness of the Creator who brought about redemption.

This might mean, as it did for Noah, that we will be out of step with the dominant stream of our culture. Though the blue sky was cloudless, Noah obeyed God and continued to build the ark, despite laughter and mockery. So, too, we must keep on offering our lives as living sacrifices to the Lord.

> Do not merely listen to the word, and so deceive your-selves. Do what it says. Anyone who listens to the word but does not do what it says is like a man who looks at his face in a mirror and, after looking at him-self, goes away and immediately forgets what he looks like. But the man who looks intently into the perfect law that gives freedom, and continues to do this, not forgetting what he has heard, but doing it—he will be blessed in what he does (James 1:22-25).

Then they will indeed know that we are Christians by our love, demonstrated in word and deed. Our neighbors will say, "Surely this is a wise and understanding people, who trust in the Lord Jesus Christ." Not for our own sakes, but for the sake of the God who "has rescued us from the dominion of darkness and brought us into the kingdom of the Son he loves," do we live.

Notes

1. Eloise Lee Leiterman, "Speedy career start top priority for private vocational schools," in *The Christian Science Monitor*, September 20, 1982, p. 18.
2. Arthur Levine, *When Dreams and Heroes Died: A Portrait of Today's College Student* (Washington, DC: Jossey-Bass Publishers, 1980), p. xvii.
3. Levine, p. 61.
4. T.J. O'Rourke, "How to Get a Good Job," in *Rolling Stone*, September 30, 1982, p. 58.
5. See a similar analysis in the field of education in chapter 5.
6. Bob Goudzwaard, *Aid for the Overdeveloped West* (Toronto: Wedge Publishing Foundation, 1975), p. 9.
7. Goudzwaard, p. 9.
8. Goudzwaard, p. 3.
9. For an elaboration on the religious roots of the economic direction of western society see Goudzwaard, pp. 16-18.
10. Goudzwaard, p. 21.

11. Goudzwaard, p. 58.
12. Dwelling House Savings and Loan Association brochure: *Meeting People's Needs* (5011 Herron Avenue, Pittsburg, Pennsylvania 15219).
13. Miki Beldman, "Thoughts on Leisure," *Vanguard*, 9, No. 4 (1979), p. 7.
14. Calvin Seerveld, *Rainbows for the Fallen World: Aesthetic Life and Artistic Task* (Toronto: Tuppence Press, 1980), p. 61.
15. Calvin Seerveld, "An Obedient Aesthetic Lifestyle," AACS Niagara Conference, August, 1981, Thompson Media, Stahlstown, Pennsylvania.
16. Seerveld, "Aesthetic Lifestyle."
17. Seerveld, "Aesthetic Lifestyle."
18. Michael Demarest, "He Digs Downtown," *Time*, August 24, 1981, p. 44.
19. Demarest, p. 44.
20. Seerveld, "Aesthetic Lifestyle."

Chapter 7

The Death of Christ and the Kingdom of God

T he good creation fell, but the fallen creation has been redeemed! The redeemed creation is being restored by
God, who works through the lives of redeemed men and
women. We can count on that restoration.

Christian men and women are servants of the Lord, living
sacrifices. Our redemption by Christ ensures our inheritance
of every good thing. We ought to live as though the creation
belongs to God our Father, and to us, because of our union
with Christ.

A view of creation redeemed by Christ gives new meaning
to the activities of everyday life. The Kingdom of God has
begun!

What Is the Kingdom of God?

The saints of the Old Testament longed for it.
John the Baptist proclaimed its imminent coming.
Jesus announced that with Him it had arrived.
Many twentieth century Christians are confused about
what it means in their lives. What is the Kingdom of God?

When this country was founded and again at the turn of
this century, many people identified the United States with
the biblical Kingdom. It looked as though it would be only a
matter of time until the perfect age was attained. However,
two world wars, a great depression, the Korean, the Viet-
namese, and the Middle Eastern "conflicts" have seriously
eroded the notion that the Kingdom of Heaven will gradually
evolve in this country or in any country on earth. Theologies
have been rewritten; most Christians in our day identify the

Kingdom anticipated by John and announced by Christ with the Kingdom of the end times. Those who hold this view await the return of Christ to inaugurate the beginning of His Kingdom.

This "future only" view, however, fails to take seriously the life and ministry of Jesus. He plainly announced the coming of the Kingdom in His own words (Luke 4:18ff), and in mighty acts such as healings (Matt. 9:1-8), casting out demons (Matt. 8:28-34), controlling nature (Mark 4:35-41), and reviving the dead (Mark 5:21-43). Most explicitly, Jesus Himself said, "But if I drive out demons by the Spirit of God, then the kingdom of God has come upon you" (Matt. 12:28). To harmonize this Kingdom-present during the life and ministry of Jesus with the "future only" view, one would have to see the death of Christ as failure, and view the history between His death and His coming again as a parenthesis which counts for nothing in eternity. Christian men and women of this age can then do nothing better than to try to survive the pilgrimage— to endure the waiting for the return of Jesus. The future-only view prevents Christians from taking part in the development and restoration of the creation which God made good. What is worse, it makes waiting comfortable: Christians cannot even see or hear the challenges before them.

Because of the difficulty they experience in being Christians in this modern world, some Christians came to view the Kingdom of God as present within their internal or private lives—and nowhere else. Christ rules their devotional times, their worship, and their morality. In his analysis of modern Christian thinking, Harry Blamires speaks to this situation:

> There is no longer a Christian mind. There is still, of course, a Christian ethic, a Christian practice, and a Christian spirituality. As a moral being, the modern Christian subscribes to a code other than that of the non-Christian. As a member of the Church, he undertakes obligations and observations ignored by the non-Christian. As a spiritual being, in prayer and meditation, he strives to cultivate a dimension of life unexplored by the non-Christian. But as a *thinking* being, the modern Christian has succumbed to secularization. He accepts religion—its morality, its worship, its spiritual culture; but he rejects the religious view of life, the view which sets all earthly issues within the context of the eternal, the view which relates all human problems—social, political,

cultural—to the doctrinal foundations of the Christian faith, the view which sees all things here below in terms of God's supremacy and earth's transitoriness, in terms of Heaven and Hell.

... My thesis amounts to this. Except over a very narrow field of thinking, chiefly touching questions of strictly personal conduct, we Christians in the modern world accept, for the purpose of mental activity, a frame of reference constructed by the secular mind and a set of criteria reflecting secular evaluations. There is no Christian mind; there is no shared field of discourse in which we can move at ease as thinking Christians by trodden ways and past established landmarks.[1]

Many who succumb to this trap eventually withdraw from the activities of normal living because they do not believe that Christ is Lord there too.

Other Christians, for centuries, have identified the Kingdom of God with the Church. Claiming that only its members are a part of the Kingdom, they have united Christ's "total" rule to one of the institutions of society. At times the Church did try to dominate all of culture, but when it failed, it retreated into itself.[2]

All of these views are deficient because they refuse to come to grips with two facts: (1) Christ inaugurated the Kingdom of God in a fresh true way during His earthly life, death, resurrection, and ascension; and (2) His Kingdom has no end. Thus, there is no dimension of life outside the rule of Christ.

Perhaps modern Christians are confused because there are not many kings today, and those we know are merely figureheads. "Kingdom" sounds like something from the past or like a fairy tale. But perhaps we can look at a modern fairy tale to recapture the meaning of the "Kingdom" concept. The *Star Wars* series is a smashing box office success.[3] Author and director, George Lucas, has attempted to reconstruct the "lost" mythological fantasy genre of film and in doing so, he has perhaps given us a medium for seeing the meaning of the Kingdom of God. Of course there are differences, notably the apparent dualism and the lack of personality in "The Force." There are distinctive differences between a biblical view of God, good and evil, and the *Star Wars* view; nevertheless, the gigantic scope of the imaginative series is instructive.

In Lucas' universe, for over a thousand generations the

Jedi Knights have been the most powerful, most respected force in the galaxy. They serve as the guardians and guarantors of peace and justice in the Old Republic (pp. 79-80). There is a "Force" in his universe, and though they have never fully defined it, scientists have theorized that it is an energy field generated by living things (p. 81). Ben (Obi-Wan) Kenobi, the last and greatest of the Jedi Knights, said, "It is an energy field and something more . . . An aura that at once controls and obeys. It is a nothingness that can accomplish miracles" (p. 120). It is the Force that gave the Jedi his special power, but the Force is dualistic, with a good and evil side. With the Jedi Knights dead or disbanded, Darth Vader used the evil side of the Force to aid corrupt emperors, and has himself risen high enough to attempt control of the universe. Luke Skywalker is instructed by Kenobi in the good side of the Force, and he joins the Alliance in opposition to Vader's attempt to conquer the universe.

Vader directs activities from a planet-like space station, the Death Star, which is "the final link in the new-forged Imperial chain which will bind the million systems of the galactic Empire together once and for all" (p. 116). The Death Star has the power to destroy an entire planet; the odds appear insurmountable for the Alliance. However, they discover "an unshielded shaft that runs directly into the main reactor system powering the station . . . A direct hit would initiate a chain reaction that will destroy the station" (p. 180). After a raging space battle, Luke uses the good side of the Force, makes a direct hit and destroys the Death Star. Darth Vader, however, escapes—to guarantee the sequel.

True, it is mythical fantasy, and yet it is instructive for us. If we see nothing more than the cosmic scope of the battle, our venture into *Star Wars* is worthwhile. The two kingdoms are battling for one universe, which is unquestionably the territory of the true Sovereign. The usurper enslaves the people until the counteroffensive is mounted. Satan has challenged God in a battle for creation, which rightly belongs to God.

The task of overcoming seems insurmountable, but the Alliance is true to the challenge. Their dedication matches their enemy's determination in the cosmic battle. If the Jedi rely on the good side of the Force for their strength and their direction, victory is sure. Just so, God's people are facing a seemingly impossible mission of creation-wide proportions and must rely on God's Spirit to direct and sustain them. The victory is sure because of the life, death, resurrection, and ascension of Christ, but there is much work still to be done.

Kingdom Firstfruits

The ministry of Jesus not only proclaimed the coming Kingdom but, even more, actually inaugurated and demonstrated the restoration that characterizes the Kingdom of God. Jesus viewed His work as a fulfillment of the Old Testament prophecy concerning the Kingdom of God. All Old Testament history centers on His Messiahship. Two kinds of kingdoms are mentioned in the Old Testament. First, there is the general Kingship of God, identified with His supremacy over all creation and over all nations throughout the world (Isaiah; Amos 1-5). This Kingship is rooted in Genesis; God has created both heaven and earth. Second, God's particular Kingship over the nation of Israel stands out. The King of the universe has a special relationship to the nation of Israel, and this focus is foremost in many parts of the Old Testament. Jesus' ministry directly fulfilled the prophetic foretelling of the Messianic King and the Servant of God—two long awaited saviors which merge in the idea of the Kingdom in the New Testament.

God's rule over the nation Israel helps to explain the New Testament idea of the Kingdom. The nation, with or without a human king, is a theocracy; God is its head. The cultic or ritualistic part of life is given prominence; all activities of life, both public and private, are subordinated to the religious. The hundreds of laws governing life showed every Jew that God was supreme in all things. No part of life was outside His domain; the best a man or woman could do was to reflect allegiance to Yahweh, the God of the Universe. Unfortunately, those points were often obscured by the interpretations given by religious leaders. Despite God's explicit and detailed teaching, neither the Jews of the Old or New Testaments nor the majority of believers today understand that God's Kingdom encompasses all of life.

Jesus transformed the national or territorial idea of Kingship. He showed how the Kingdom is the exercise of God's reign in creation. He put forth His power in natural and supernatural acts of salvation. In this way Jesus inaugurates the Kingdom of God, and will complete it when He returns. Christian men and women today live between the time of the Kingdom's beginning and its completion. Christ's Kingdom began as a series of conquests and the process of those conquests will continue until He returns to finish the work.

Christ's Kingdom Is Begun

There is a close association in the Hebrew mind between the coming of the Messiah and the coming of the Kingdom. Both the Kingdom of God and the restoration of Israel are anticipated in the proclamation of the Messiah-King in the Gospel according to Luke (1:32, 33). Mary's hymn (the Magnificat) sings of the divine grace shown to her and of God's pity on His people (Luke 1:46-55). Zechariah praises God for visiting and redeeming His people by bringing salvation from the house of David (Luke 1:68ff). The song of the angels announces the birth of Christ: "glory to God in the highest," and "peace on earth," picturing the final bliss of the Kingdom that is beginning. There is indeed a geographical element in the Messiah's reign, but the Messiah will be begotten by the Holy Spirit (Luke 1:33-35) and His Kingdom will have no end.

John the Baptist's preaching confirms the Messianic element of the Kingdom, and he pictures a Kingdom which carries with it transcendent and universal judgment (Matt. 11:3; Luke 7:19), calling it "the coming wrath" (Matt. 3:7). John's preaching also contains the twofold meaning of the Kingdom which is coming: Those whom God will redeem will be given an unsurpassed measure of the Spirit, and those who will be lost are abandoned to the torture of fire (cf. Matt. 3:11, 12).

Jesus only rarely speaks of Himself as the Christ or Messiah (Matt. 24:5); rather, the reference "Son of Man" occupies a prominent place in His preaching of the coming of the Kingdom. In the synoptic Gospels, "the coming of the Son of Man" and "the coming of the Kingdom of God" are often synonymous (Matt. 13:41 and Mark 9:1). Jesus speaks of the Kingdom of the Son of Man (Matt. 13:41; 16:28); of the Son of Man sitting in His glorious throne in the regeneration (Matt. 19:28); of the sign of the Son of Man (Matt. 24:30); of ". . . the Son of Man sitting at the right hand of the Mighty One and coming on the clouds of heaven" (Matt. 26:64); and proclaims that His glory is that of His Father and holy angels (Luke 9:26). Divine judgment, authority, and the coming of the Kingdom have all been placed in the hands of the Son of Man. As Daniel 7 confirms, the Son of Man is not an ordinary man clothed with temporary national power. Rather, He is a universal and transcendent person who has been given unlimited authority and has been entrusted with God's dominion. The Son of Man and the Messiah-King are one. Jesus unifies these concepts explicitly in His reference to Himself as both Lord and Son

(Matt. 22:42, 43). However, the Davidic Messiah-King and Son of Man is also the Suffering Servant of the Lord. Jesus the Messiah had to fulfill, in complete submission to the will of the Father, the task given Him. That task began with His temple visit at age twelve (Luke 2:49), continued through the wilderness temptation and His preaching of the Kingdom (Luke 4:1-21), and culminated in His suffering and death.

Jesus preached the Kingdom in words and in deeds. His miracles illustrated that the "new age" existed simultaneously with the old; they are visible examples of restoration. They demonstrate that the Kingdom, and hence the restoration, is creation-wide. The miracles manifest the authority of Jesus and, more importantly for our purpose here, they demonstrate the restoration which Christ's Kingdom brings to all of life. Both supernatural and natural forces submit to His command. Furthermore, Jesus' power over satan displays the cosmic scope of the Kingdom, and His own absolute reign. The casting out of demons proves that Jesus has indeed won the victory. Jesus' power over satan is illustrated from the time of the wilderness temptation and throughout His ministry (Matt. 8:29; Mark 1:34, 3:11; Luke 4:34, 8:28). In Jesus' person and His coming, the Kingdom has present reality. Satan's fall from heaven (Luke 10:18, 19) is the beginning of the end for the devil's kingdom; the Kingdom of God has come.

> . . . all that Jesus did and suffered in obeying God's commands was part and parcel of his messianic office in the full sense of the term. And in all this the kingdom had come. The world of God's redemption was not only revealed in Jesus' power over the Evil One, in his miracles, in his authoritative preaching of salvation. It was no less revealed and present in the perfect obedience of the Servant of the Lord to the will of the Father, in his taking upon himself the infirmities of his people, in his substitutionary self-sacrifice as a ransom for many. This is the thought of the mediator who fulfills the law, offers the sacrifice, expiates the guilt; and representing the people in this, thus redeems them. This, too, is the kingdom of heaven.[4]

Continue Until the Fullness

The Kingdom continues, that Kingdom begun by Jesus' life, ministry, death, resurrection, and ascension. Christian men and women live in the middle of it, and their lives should show the difference.

We are servants of the King of all creation; this must be reflected in everything we do.[5] What is more, Christians are those to whom the task of restoration has been given. His children are not aliens visiting a strange land; they are the citizens; theirs is the responsibility to restore what God has created. As agents of reconciliation, they are to bring restoration to every aspect of the creation. All areas or structures can be restored in Christ. What Jesus began through His own ministry, His followers are to continue until He comes. Restored to the men and women God created us to be, they carry restoration into family, work, play, and society. What began with the ministry of Jesus is continued through the patient, obedient lives of His people. Though we seem like grasshoppers before the task, we know that "the Lord is with us" (Num. 13:26—14:12). The work seems overwhelming, "but those who hope in the Lord will renew their strength. They will soar on wings like eagles . . ." and never grow weary or faint (Is. 40:31).

Never may His people grow proud of their efforts, as if they will bring about the fullness of the Kingdom themselves. His people merely live obediently by His grace, relying on the direction of the Holy Spirit to restore what has deteriorated. Before the completion of His Kingdom, He will return to add the finishing touches. What He began and His people continue, only He can complete. Just as we can rely only upon Him for our salvation, we can rely only upon Him to complete the Kingdom He began. However, our responsibility to work actively for restoration is clear.[6]

Every Day in Every Way

We were bought with a price while we were in the depth of our sin. Jesus cannot be our friend without being our Lord and Redeemer. Redemption is as wide as all creation. Hence, the Kingdom of God is much more than a theological idea which we affirm while sitting in the pew. Rather, it is the foundation upon which our lives must be lived.

Christian faith is relevant for our times—as we will learn as we work out redemption in our families, our teaching, our studying, our politics, our businesses, and every area of daily life. If our lives are divided—Sunday faith versus daily living—we will at some point throw up our hands in despair and either forsake our faith in Christ because it doesn't relate to the normal activities of our daily life, or we will retreat in some way to escape everyday life, or worse, we will continue to live the divided life. Twentieth century men and women must see active demonstrations that redemption in Christ has implications in the mill as well as the church, in the university as well as the seminary, and in recreation and the marketplace as well as Bible study. Pastors must help their congregations see the meaning of their Christian faith for seven days each week. Parents must teach their children that all of life belongs to God, and that everything that they do should give honor and glory to Him.

If modern Christians fail in this task, their lives will remain fractured. Broken people look for relief from pressures and responsibilities. They cannot accept the challenge of restoring the creation which God called good.

Being a whole Christian means knowing the implications of our salvation in everything we do. It means not limiting our faith to morality or relationships, but expanding it to encompass the product we sell and the political party we endorse, as well as the house we buy (or the neighborhood it is in), and the school or bank we support. Christian lives built in this way withstand pressure and the test of time because they are woven as one fabric, without seam or tear; there is marvelous consistency between belief and life.

The life, death, resurrection and ascension of Christ announces the Kingdom of God. His redeemed people are empowered to demonstrate the power of that redemption throughout the creation. Nothing exists which lies beyond the rule of Christ. The task of Christian men and women today is to recognize the impact of the Lordship of Christ in their own lives, and in so doing, to demonstrate that all things are in the process of restoration in Christ.

Notes

1. Harry Blamires, *The Christian Mind: How Should A Christian Think?* (Ann Arbor: Servant Books, 1978), p. 4.
2. There is another form of "Church-Kingdom" view which identifies the Church with the "elect." Often these people refuse to see the scope of the Kingdom of God outside of the spiritual lives of believers and their roles within the visible Church. Essentially this results in the same retreat

into itself already identified with this narrow "Church-Kingdom" view.

3. George Lucas, *Star Wars: from the Adventures of Luke Skywalker* (New York: Ballantine Books, 1976).

4. Herman Ridderbos, *The Coming of the Kingdom*, trans. by H. de Jongste, ed. by Raymond O. Zorn (Philadelphia: Presbyterian and Reformed Publishing Company, 1962, 1969), p. 171.

5. See Chapter 3 of this work for our elaboration of this subject.

6. See Chapter 4 of this work for our elaboration of this subject.

For Further Reading

Blamires, Harry, *The Christian Mind*, Servant Books, Ann Arbor, Michigan, 1963.

De Graaf, S.G., *Promise and Deliverance*, Vols. 1-4, Paideia Press, St. Catharines, Ontario, 1977.

Diehl, William E., *Thank God, It's Monday*, Fortress Press, Philadelphia, 1982.

Goudzwaard, Bob, *Capitalism and Progress*, Wedge Publishing Foundation, Toronto, and William B. Eerdmans Publishing Co., Grand Rapids, 1979.

Kuyper, Abraham, *Lectures on Calvinism*, William B. Eerdmans Publishing Co., Grand Rapids, 1931.

McCarthy, Rockne M., James W. Skillen, William A. Harper, *Disestablishment a Second Time*, Christian University Press, Grand Rapids, 1982.

Mouw, Richard J., *Called to Holy Worldliness*, Fortress Press, Philadelphia, 1980.

Ridderbos, Herman, *The Coming of the Kingdom*, The Presbyterian and Reformed Publishing Co., Philadelphia, 1962.

Runner, H. Evan, *The Relation of the Bible to Learning*, Paideia Press, Jordan Station, Ontario, 1982, revised edition.

Schaeffer, Francis A., *Escape From Reason*, Inter-Varsity Press, Downers Grove, 1968.

Seerveld, Calvin, *Rainbows For the Fallen World*, Tuppence Press, Toronto, 1980.

Storkey, Alan, *A Christian Social Perspective*, Inter-Varsity Press, Leicester, England, 1979.

To Prod the "Slumbering Giant": Crisis Commitment and Christian Education, Wedge Publishing Foundation, Toronto, 1972.

Walsh, Brian, and Richard Middleton, *Quest for an Authentic Life*, Inter-Varsity Press, Downers Grove, to be published, 1984.

Wilkinson, Loren (ed.), *Earthkeeping*, William B. Eerdmans Publishing Co., Grand Rapids, 1980.

Wolters, Al, *Biblical Basics for a Reformational World View* (forthcoming publication).